MW00962094

THE INFANCY
GOSPELS

Exploring Jesus' Family

THE INFANCY GOSPELS

Exploring Jesus' Family

by Mark M. Mattison

Also by Mark M. Mattison

The Gospel of Mary:
A Fresh Translation and Holistic Approach

The Gospel of Judas:
The Sarcastic Gospel

The Gospel of Thomas:
A New Translation for Spiritual Seekers

The Gospel of Q:
Jesus' Prophetic Wisdom

The Gospel of Philip:
The Divine Mysteries of Marriage and Rebirth

The Gospel of Peter:
Revisiting Jesus' Death and Resurrection

The Gospel of Truth:
The Mystical Gospel

For more information, visit:
http://www.gospels.net

First Edition

© 2019 Mark M. Mattison. All rights reserved.

Scripture quotations marked DFV are from the *Divine Feminine Version* (DFV) of the New Testament, made publicly available through the Creative Commons License – Attribution, Noncommercial, Share Alike 3.0 United States. For full details see:
http://creativecommons.org/licenses/by-nc-sa/3.0/us

Contents

Acknowledgements

I'd like to express my gratitude to all the women and men of the Grand Rapids Writer's Exchange who have played such an important role in my journey as a writer over the last twelve years. Their constructive criticism of my writing has been invaluable.

Thanks are specifically due to Samuel Zinner, Wes Thompson, Princess O'Nika Auguste, Debbie Burnham-Kidwell, and Lareta Finger. Of course, I remain solely responsible for any errors or mistakes.

Finally, I'm deeply grateful to my wife, Rebecca, whose graceful and patient encouragement is a source of inexhaustible spiritual strength.

Introduction

Late in 2017, in the run-up to a special election for the United States Senate, allegations emerged that a leading candidate had approached minors for sex when he was in his thirties. A state politician shockingly dismissed the accusations with the statement, "take Joseph and Mary. Mary was a teenager and Joseph was an adult carpenter. They became parents of Jesus. There's just nothing immoral or illegal here."[1]

Apart from the fact that the tradition about Joseph and Mary was cited far out of context ("Their whole deal is that there was no funny business!" quipped a late night talk show host), where did it come from? None of the Gospels in the New Testament mention the ages of Joseph and Mary, yet many have heard that Joseph was an old man and Mary only sixteen years old. Biblical scholars took note, however, knowing exactly where that tradition came from: a second-century text known as the Infancy Gospel of James.

Some years earlier, in 2000, a television movie about Jesus[2] depicted another tradition not found in the New Testament: A young Jesus bringing a dead sparrow to life. There's no story like that in Matthew, Mark, Luke, or John, but there is a story about the young Jesus giving life to clay sparrows in the Infancy Gospel of Thomas.

Though not widely circulated as part of the New Testament, these two little-known Infancy Gospels have been far more influential in the development of Christian thought than many realize. Unlike other extracanonical Gospels, they were not lost to history and rediscovered or reconstructed within the last hundred years. Originally written in the second century, they've been copied and read throughout the history of the Church.

Traditionally, many have approached these Infancy Gospels as second-rate curiosities, popular books of less value than the New Testament Gospels. They've too often been interpreted as little more than combinations of the infancy narratives of Matthew and Luke, fleshing out a plausible back-story of Jesus' family – thereby "filling in the blanks," as it were – for a curious Christian audience. As Christopher Frilingos writes, "In the past, scholars often dismissed these gospels as tabloid accounts meant to satisfy a craving for tidbits about the celebrities of the faith."[3]

Today, however, scholars are taking these texts more seriously, asking what they may have meant to their early readers and how they've shaped Christian tradition. These Gospels did more than simply reiterate older stories and add superfluous details. On the contrary, they did exactly what other narrative Gospels did: they built upon prior tradition and reframed it in new ways for the faith communities of their time – for better *and* for worse.

As we'll see in Chapter One, Infancy James features women as key characters – Anna, Mary, Elizabeth, and midwives – but its intense concern for Mary's perpetual virginity reinforced unhealthy attitudes toward women. Bettina Eltrop and Claudia Janssen write that Infancy James:

> has no interest in the life of women who do not stand in the immediate context of their reproductive capabilities and of questions about their sexuality. The emphasis on virginity here also fails to offer women any perspectives for an autonomous and independent life.[4]

On the other hand, this Gospel is noteworthy for its deference to Jewish traditions and institutions, especially the Temple, holding out hope for its restoration.[5]

By contrast, Infancy Thomas presents Jews as adversarial, prefiguring the canonical Gospels' depiction of Jesus' conflicts with the Pharisees. What's most shocking about Infancy Thomas is its portrayal of the child Jesus as capricious and insensitive, which requires some theological unpacking in Chapter Three.

Like many other narrative Gospels, then, the Infancy Gospels are a "mixed bag": carefully-shaped stories that contain both uplifting spiritual insight *as well as* unhealthy social attitudes. But given their long history of influence in the Christian Church, a critical reevaluation of these ancient texts can help us better to appreciate their meaning and place in the history of the church.

1
Exploring the Infancy Gospel of James

Ancient manuscripts of Infancy James have been preserved in Arabic, Armenian, Coptic, Ethiopic, Georgian, Latin, and Syriac, but most – around 140 manuscripts – are in Greek.[1] Scholars agree it was originally written in Greek in the second century,[2] and many believe it was written in Syria.[3] It's most commonly described by the Latin title under which it was introduced to the West – the *Protevangelium Jacobi,* or the "Proto-Gospel of James." This title positions it as a "prequel" to the Gospels about Jesus.[4] Interestingly, the earliest Greek manuscript, the Bodmer Papyrus which dates to the late third or early fourth century, is titled "Birth of Mary, Apocalypse of James."

The first part of that title, "Birth of Mary," should come as little surprise to those who are familiar with its contents. Most of this Gospel is a story about Mary: It starts with her parents, Joachim and Anna (chapters 1-4), and goes on to narrate Mary's birth (chapter 5), childhood (chapters 6 and 7), betrothal to Joseph (chapters 8 and 9), work in the Temple (chapter 10), miraculous conception (chapters 11-17), and finally the virgin birth of her son, Jesus (chapters 18-21). The second part of the title, however, may seem more puzzling. In what sense can this Gospel be understood as an "Apocalypse" or Revelation, a text about persecution and divine deliverance?

This question highlights a lesser-known aspect of this Gospel. Samuel Zinner writes:

> At times some scholars perhaps have overemphasized Mary's role in [Infancy James], inadequately appreciating the

predominating role of the Jerusalem temple, the setting of the text's main plot basically from beginning to end. [Its] second sentence (1:1's gifts offered to the Lord) presupposes the temple, and the final stories in chs. 23-24, Zechariah's murder and his priestly replacement, take place in the temple (ch. 23 explicitly so, ch. 24 implicitly). [Infancy James] was composed by a Christian with a noticeably positive disposition towards Jews and the temple.[5]

Indeed, the slaughter of the infants and the miraculous deliverance of Elizabeth and her son John (chapter 22), as well as the martyrdom of Zechariah (chapters 23 and 24) and the flight into the wilderness "until the commotion in Jerusalem had died down" (chapter 25; cf. Mark 13:14 pars.; Rev. 12:6) all resonate with apocalyptic warnings.[6] Ironic precursors of the temple veil's rending (chapters 10 and 24) and the destruction of the temple (chapter 24) intensify the second-century hope for its restoration.[7] But these aren't the only aspects of Infancy James that reflect strong concern for Jewish traditions and institutions.

Another Jewish feature of Infancy James is its use of "midrash," a way of building new narratives using familiar Scriptural stories. For example, Anna's lament about her childlessness in chapters 2 and 3 evokes the stories of Sarah, Elizabeth, Hannah, and Judith. Like Hannah, Anna dedicated her child to God.[8] Examples like this may be multiplied many times over. In this way, as Bettina Eltrop and Claudia Jannsen put it:

> People who heard these stories immediately had in view the images and events of the biblical stories they knew: the fateful experiences of childless foremothers and forefathers, the fortunate turn of events for Israel in the account about Judith, the story of Susanna and the Hannah-Samuel tradition, the fate of Zechariah in 2 Chronicles.[9]

Though some scholars tend to think of Infancy James as fundamentally misunderstanding Judaism, others, like Megan

Nutzman, have demonstrated that it reflects several Jewish traditions.[10] Zinner concurs, writing that "Despite some claims that [Infancy James] is thoroughly pagan and Hellenistic in its contents, scholars increasingly recognize that it does preserve at least some accurate Jewish or so-called Jewish-Christian traditions."[11]

In fact, the only passage which *could* be read as anti-Jewish is a single statement in chapter 24: "Zechariah has been murdered, and his blood won't be wiped away until his avenger comes!" This readily brings to mind Matthew 23:29-38, which depicts the desolation of the temple as a punishment of Jews per se. But as Zinner points out, 2 Chronicles 24:22 provides a more likely context: The vengeance meted out through the agency of malevolent Roman invaders reflects the punishment of the invading Syrians in 2 Chronicles 24:23-25.[12] "On the face of it," Zinner writes, Infancy James 24 "is anti-Herodian, not anti-Jewish. ... In itself there is nothing anti-Jewish about awaiting an avenger for the murder of a Jewish priest."[13]

Other midrashic elements color the nativity story.[14] In Infancy James chapter 19, a midwife comes "down from the mountain," as does Moses in Exodus 19. Similarly, a "bright cloud overshadowed the cave" in which Mary was giving birth, calling to mind God coming in "a dense cloud" in Exodus 19:9. In addition to the overshadowing cloud, "a great light" calls to mind the "thunder and lightning" in Exodus 19:16 when limits are set around Mount Sinai so that it isn't to be touched on pain of death (Exod. 19:12ff). Similarly, consuming fire emerges from the ark of the covenant in Leviticus 10:2.

Mary is like the consecrated "Holy of Holies,"[15] surrounded by a dense cloud like Sinai and carrying the fire of God's presence like the ark of the covenant – easily explaining Salome's injury when she attempts to examine Mary, whose "body becomes a channel of holy power. She is a sacred vessel, and this makes her dangerous. A divine fire continues to burn inside Mary after the baby has exited."[16]

This infancy narrative draws just as deeply from the tradition of the canonical Gospels. For example, the "great light" in the cave recalls the narrative of Jesus' transfiguration.[17] And Salome's visit to Jesus in a cave at his birth recalls another Salome's visit to another cave associated with a different Joseph (of Arimathea) at the other end of Jesus' life.[18]

However, the motif of the virgin birth in Infancy James demonstrates a significant (and more detrimental) development from the New Testament Gospels. Jane Schaberg argues that the author's intent was to counter polemic regarding the virgin birth, but that "the long-range effect was to foster male regulation of female virgins."[19]

Ironically, despite the fact that Mary is this Gospel's central character, the reader rarely gets a glimpse of Mary's inner thoughts. From her birth, to her childhood, to the annunciation, she's provided a single path, to which she simply acquiesces. The reader is privy to few of her inner deliberations. By contrast, Joseph's inner dialogue takes up much of chapters 13 and 14. Mary's mother, Anna, also expresses her inner thoughts (especially in chapter 3), but only with respect to her reproductive role. As Schaberg puts it:

> Although *Proto-James* focuses on female characters, male interests predominate. There is no clear evidence of a female point of view or distinctively female preoccupations, thoughts, or feelings; no interest in the female apart from the male (including the male God), or in aspects of women's lives not connected with sexuality.[20]

In sum, Infancy James is a more complex and nuanced theological Gospel than many have realized, and it's receiving more serious attention from scholars as a significant work in its own right. Like many other early texts composed by Jesus' followers, it influenced the development of the Christian Church far beyond what its original author and later editors ever imagined, for better and for worse.

About This Translation

The new translation in Chapter Two is more colloquial than the more literal version in Appendix A. Chapter breaks and titles are not original to the text, but follow standard divisions used in other translations. Parentheses denote editorial insertions to clarify the meaning of the text. For more information about the manuscript tradition, see Appendix A.

2
The Infancy Gospel of James
A New Translation

Chapter 1: Joachim's Plight

Joachim was a very rich man in the histories of the twelve tribes of Israel. He doubled the gifts he offered to the Lord. "One is from my surplus for all the people," he said to himself, "and the other is my atonement to the Lord God for forgiveness."

Now the great day of the Lord was coming, and the people of Israel were offering their gifts. But Reubel stood in his way. "It's not right for you to offer your gifts first," he objected, "since you haven't had a child in Israel."

Joachim was very upset. He went to the (history) of the twelve tribes of the people. "I'll look in the (history) of the twelve tribes of Israel," he said to himself, "to see whether I'm the only one who hasn't had a child in Israel." When he searched, he found that all the just people in Israel had raised children. He remembered that in the last days of the patriarch Abraham, the Lord God gave him a son, Isaac.

Joachim was very upset. He didn't go to his wife, but went off into the wilderness instead and pitched his tent there. Joachim fasted forty days and forty nights. "I won't go down to eat or drink until the Lord my God considers my plight," he said to himself. "Prayer will be my only food and drink."

Chapter 2: Anna's Plight

Now Anna, his wife, mourned and lamented for two reasons. "I lament that I'm a widow," she said, "and that I don't have a child."

Now the great day of the Lord was coming. Her servant Juthine asked her, "How long are you going to humiliate yourself? Look, the great day of the Lord has come, and you shouldn't be upset. But take this headband which my manager gave me. It's not right for me to wear it, since I'm your servant, and it bears a royal mark."

But Anna said, "Get away from me! I won't do this. The Lord God has really humiliated me. Maybe a trickster gave this to you, and you're trying to get me to join you in your wrongdoing."

"Why should I curse you," asked Juthine the servant, "since you haven't heard a word I've said? The Lord God has made you infertile, to give you no fruit in Israel."

Anna was very upset. She removed her mourning garment, washed her face, and put on her wedding dress. And at about three o'clock she went down into her garden to walk around. She saw a laurel tree and sat under it. After resting, she petitioned the Lord. "God of my ancestors," she said, "bless me and hear my prayer, as you blessed our mother Sarah and gave her a son, Isaac."

Chapter 3: Anna's Lament

Anna looked intently to heaven and saw a nest of sparrows in the laurel tree. Anna lamented. She said to herself:

"I'm so sad! Who gave birth to me? Who bore me? I was born as a curse before the people of Israel. They've mocked me and banished me from the Temple of the Lord my God.

"I'm so sad! What am I like? I'm not like the birds of heaven, because even the birds of heaven are productive before you, Lord.

"I'm so sad! What am I like? I'm not like the animals, because even the animals are productive before you, Lord.

"I'm so sad! What am I like? I'm not like the wild animals of the earth, because even the wild animals of the earth are productive before you, Lord.

"I'm so sad! What am I like? I'm not like these waters, because even these waters are serene yet churn, and their fish bless you, Lord.

"I'm so sad! What am I like? I'm not like this earth, because even this earth produces its fruits when it's time and blesses you, Lord.

Chapter 4: The Lord's Promise

And look! An angel of the Lord stood nearby. "Anna, Anna," it said, "the Lord has heard your prayer. You'll conceive and give birth, and your child will be talked about throughout the whole world."

"As the Lord God lives," Anna said, "whether I have a boy or a girl, I'll bring the child as a gift to the Lord my God, and it will minister to God all the days of its life."

And look! Two angels came. "Look," they said to her, "your husband Joachim is coming with his flocks." Because an angel of the Lord had gone down to Joachim and told him, "Joachim, Joachim, the Lord God has heard your prayer. Go down from here. Look, Anna, your wife, has conceived."

Joachim went down right away and called the shepherds. "Bring me ten lambs without spot or blemish," he told them. "The ten lambs will be for the Lord God. And bring twelve tender calves for the priests and the elders. Finally, bring a hundred male goats for all the people."

And look! Joachim came with his shepherds. Anna stood at the gate. When she saw Joachim coming with his flocks, she immediately ran and flung herself around his neck. "Now I know that the Lord God has greatly blessed me," Anna said. "Because look! The widow is no longer a widow, and look! The one without a child has conceived."

So Joachim rested for the first day he was home.

Chapter 5: Mary's Birth

And the next day, he was offering his gifts. "If the Lord God is really reconciled to me," he said to himself, "I'll see it reflected in the metal plate on the priest's turban." So Joachim offered his gifts and paid attention to the priest's metal plate as he went up to the Lord's altar. He didn't see any wrongdoing reflected in it.

"Now I know," Joachim said, "that the Lord God has been reconciled to me and has forgiven me all my wrongdoings." And he went down from the Lord's Temple justified and went into his house.

After Anna was pregnant about six months, she gave birth in her seventh month. "Is it a boy or a girl?" she asked her midwife.

"It's a girl!"

"I'm so thrilled!" Anna exclaimed, laying down her child.

When the time came, Anna cleansed her menstrual flow, breastfed her child, and named her Mary.

Chapter 6: Mary's First Year

And the child grew stronger every day. When she was six months old, her mother stood her on the ground to see whether she could stand. After walking seven steps, she went to her mother's breast. Her mother caught her up and said, "As the Lord my God lives, you won't walk on this ground again until I bring you into the Lord's Temple!"

So she made a sanctuary in her bedroom and didn't allow anything sacrilegious or impure to pass through it. And she called the pure daughters of the Hebrews to play with her.

And when she got to be a year old, Joachim threw a great feast. He invited the chief priests, the priests, the scribes, the elders, and all the people of Israel. And Joachim presented the child to the priests. They blessed her. "God of our ancestors," they said, "bless this child. May her name be spoken forever among all generations."

All the people answered, "So be it. Amen!"

And they presented her to the chief priests. They blessed her too. "Most High God," they said, "Look upon this child, and give her an ultimate blessing that can't be surpassed."

Then her mother took her up to the sanctuary of her bedroom and breastfed her. Anna sang a song to the Lord God:

"I'll sing a holy song to the Lord my God, because God has visited me, and has removed the criticism of my enemies.

"And the Lord God has given me the fruit of God's justice, both singular and manifold before God.

"Who will report to Reubel's people that Anna nurses a child? 'Listen up, listen up, twelve tribes of Israel: Anna nurses a child!'"

Anna rested in the sanctuary of her bedroom. Then she went and ministered to her guests. When they finished dinner, they left, rejoicing and glorifying Israel's God.

Chapter 7: Mary Goes to the Temple

She cared for her child through the months. When she turned two, Joachim said, "Let's take her to the Lord's Temple to keep our promise, so that the Lord won't be angry at us and find our gift unacceptable."

But Anna said, "Let's wait until she's three, so that she won't miss her father or mother."

"Alright, we'll wait," Joachim agreed.

When the child turned three, Joachim said, "Let's call the pure daughters of the Hebrews. Let them take their lamps and light them, so that the child won't turn back, and her heart won't be drawn away from the Lord's Temple." And that's what they did until they went up to the Lord's Temple.

The priest welcomed her and kissed her. "The Lord God has magnified your name among all the generations," he said. "Through you, the Lord will reveal the redemption of the people of Israel in the last days."

He sat her down on the third step of the altar, and the Lord God showered her with grace. She danced on her feet, and everyone in Israel loved her.

Chapter 8: Mary Turns Twelve

Her parents went home, marveling, praising, and glorifying the Lord God that their child hadn't turned back. While she was in the Lord's Temple, Mary was nurtured like a dove, and was fed by an angel's hand.

When she turned twelve, the priests held a council. "Look," they said, "Mary has been in the Lord's Temple for twelve years. What should we do about her so that she won't pollute the sanctuary of the Lord our God?" They said to the chief priest, "You stand at the Lord's altar. Go in and pray about her, and whatever the Lord God reveals to you, we'll do it."

So the chief priest went in, taking the robe with twelve bells into the Holy of Holies, and prayed about her. 7And look! An angel of the Lord stood nearby. "Zechariah, Zechariah," it said, "go out and assemble the widowers of the people. Let each of them bring a staff. Whomever the Lord God points out with a sign, she'll be his wife."

So the heralds went out through the whole surrounding area of Judea, sounding the Lord's trumpet. And look! All the men rushed in.

Chapter 9: Joseph Protects Mary

Joseph threw down his axe too, and went to the meeting. When they had all gathered, they went to the priest with their staffs. And having taken all their staffs, he went into the Temple and prayed. When he had finished the prayer, he took the staffs, went out, and gave them back. But there wasn't a sign among them. Joseph took his last, and look! A dove emerged from the staff, and flew onto Joseph's head. The priest told Joseph, "You've been chosen to take care of the Lord's virgin."

But Joseph refused. "I have sons and am an old man," he said, "but she's young! I won't be a joke among the people of Israel."

The priest replied, "Joseph, fear the Lord your God, and remember what God did to Dathan, Abiron, and Kore; how the earth opened and swallowed all of them because of their rebellion. So be careful, Joseph, that these things don't happen in your house."

Afraid, Joseph welcomed her into his care. "Mary," he told her, "I've taken you from the Lord's Temple, and now I'm bringing you to my house. I'm going away to build houses, but I'll come back to you. Meanwhile, the Lord will protect you."

Chapter 10: The Temple Veil

Now the priests held a council. They said, "Let's make a veil for the Lord's Temple."

The priest said, "Call the pure virgins from the tribe of David to me." So the officers went out, searched, and found seven virgins. Then the priest remembered that the child Mary was from the tribe of David and pure before God. So the officers went out and brought her.

They brought them into the Lord's Temple. The priest said, "Cast lots for me to see who will spin the gold, the white, the linen, the silk, the violet, the scarlet, and the true purple."

The lot for the true purple and scarlet fell to Mary, so she took them back to her house. This was the same time that Zechariah fell silent, and Samuel replaced him until Zechariah could speak. Meanwhile, Mary took the scarlet and spun it.

Chapter 11: The Angel Appears to Mary

She took the pitcher and went to fill it with water, and look! A voice told her, "Rejoice, blessed one! The Lord is with you. You're blessed among women."

Mary looked around right and left to see where the voice might be coming from. Terrified, she went back to her house. Setting down the pitcher, she sat on her throne, took up the purple, and spun it.

And look! An angel of the Lord stood before her, saying, "Don't be afraid, Mary, because you've found grace before the Lord of All. You'll conceive from God's word."

When she heard this, Mary questioned herself. "Will I conceive from the Lord, the living God," she asked, "and give birth like all other women give birth?"

"Not like that, Mary," the angel of the Lord said, "because God's power will overshadow you, so the holy one to whom you'll give birth will be called the Son of the Most High. You'll name him 'Jesus,' because he'll save his people from their wrongdoings.

"Look," Mary replied, "I'm the servant of the Lord. May what you've said come true."

Chapter 12: Mary Visits Elizabeth

She finished the purple and the scarlet and took it to the priest. When he took it, the priest blessed her. "Mary," he said, "the Lord God has magnified your name, and you'll be blessed among all the generations of the earth."

Mary rejoiced and went to visit her cousin Elizabeth. She knocked at the door. When Elizabeth heard her, she flung down the scarlet, rushed to the door, and opened it. She blessed her: "How is it that the mother of my Lord should come to me? Look, the unborn one in me leaped and blessed you!"

But Mary forgot the mysteries which the angel Gabriel had told her. She looked intently into heaven. "Lord, who am I," she asked, "that all the women of the earth will bless me?"

She spent three months with Elizabeth. Every day, her womb grew larger. Afraid, Mary went back home and hid herself from the people of Israel. She was only sixteen when these mysterious things happened to her.

Chapter 13: Joseph Questions Mary

She was sixth months pregnant, and look! Joseph returned from his construction work, came into the house, and found her pregnant. He struck himself in the face and flung himself on the ground in sackcloth, weeping bitterly. "How can I show my face to the Lord God?" he asked. "What can I pray about this young girl, since I took her as a virgin from the Lord God's Temple and didn't protect her? Who has set this trap for me? Who has done this evil thing in my house? Who has violated the virgin? Aren't I reliving the story of Adam? As Adam was glorifying God in the hour of prayer, the serpent came, found Eve alone, and deceived her. And now it's happened to me!"

Then Joseph stood from the sackcloth and called her. "God cared for you," he said. "What have you done? You've forgotten the Lord your God. Why have you humiliated yourself? You were nourished in the Holy of Holies and were fed by an angel's hand!"

She wept bitterly. "I'm pure," she replied, "and I haven't slept with any man!"

So Joseph said to her, "Then where did this thing in your womb come from?"

"As the Lord my God lives," she replied, "I don't know where it came from!"

Chapter 14: Joseph's Dream

Joseph was very afraid. He kept quiet, considering what to do about her. Joseph said, "If I hide her wrongdoing, I'll be found resisting the Lord's law; but if I expose her to the people of Israel, I'm afraid that what's inside her might be angelic, and I'll be found handing over innocent blood to the judgment of death. So what will I do about her? I'll secretly set her free from me."

Then night overtook him. And look! An angel of the Lord appeared to him in a dream. "Don't be afraid of this child," it said, "because the one in her is from the Holy Spirit. She'll give birth to a son, and you'll name him 'Jesus,' because he'll save his people from their wrongdoings."

Then Joseph got up from his sleep and glorified the God of Israel, who had given him grace. And he protected her.

Chapter 15: The Chief Priest Questions Mary and Joseph

Then Annas the scribe came to him. "Joseph," he asked, "why haven't you come to our traveling group?"

He replied, "Because I was worn out from the trip and rested my first day back."

Then Annas turned and saw Mary pregnant.

So he went straight to the priest. "Joseph," he said, "about whom you bore witness, has broken the law."

"What?" asked the chief priest.

"Remember the virgin that Joseph took from the Lord's Temple?" he asked. "He's violated her. He's stolen her wedding and hasn't revealed it to the people of Israel."

The priest asked, "Joseph did this?"

"Send officers," Annas replied, "and you'll find the virgin pregnant."

Then the officers went and found her just as he said. So they took her and Joseph to court.

"Mary," the chief priest asked, "why have you done this? Why have you humiliated yourself and forgotten the Lord your God? You were raised in the Holy of Holies and were fed by an angel's hand. You heard its hymns and danced for it. What have you done?"

She wept bitterly. "As the Lord God lives," she said, "I'm pure before God, and I haven't slept with any man!"

Then the priest said, "Joseph, what have you done?"

"As the Lord my God lives," Joseph said, "and as the witness of God's truth, I haven't touched her!"

"Don't perjure yourself, but tell the truth," the priest said. "You stole her wedding and didn't reveal it to the people of Israel, and you haven't submitted to the mighty hand that should bless your offspring."

Joseph fell silent.

Chapter 16: The Test

The chief priest said, "Return the virgin you took from the Lord's Temple."

Joseph became tearful.

Then the priest said, "I'll give you the water of the Lord's rebuke to drink, and it'll reveal your wrongdoing to you."

Taking the water, the priest gave it to Joseph and sent him into the wilderness. But Joseph returned unharmed.

Then he gave it to Mary and sent her into the wilderness. She returned unharmed, too.

All the people were amazed that their wrongdoing wasn't revealed.

"If the Lord God hasn't revealed your wrongdoing to you," said the priest, "then I don't judge you either." Then he let them go free.

Joseph took Mary and went home, rejoicing and glorifying the God of Israel.

Chapter 17: The Census

Now an order went out from Augustus the king to register the number of people in Bethlehem of Judea.

Joseph said, "I'll register my sons. But what should I do about this child? How will I register her? As my wife? I'm ashamed to do that. As my daughter? But the people of Israel know she's not my daughter. This is the Lord's day; I'll do whatever the Lord wants."

So he saddled the donkey and sat her on it. His son led it, and Samuel followed behind.

When they got three miles down the road, Joseph turned around and saw that she was sad. He thought, "Likely the one inside her is causing her discomfort."

Joseph turned around again and saw her laughing. "Mary," he asked her, "What's with you? First I see you laughing, but then sad?"

"It's because I see two people," she replied. "One is crying and mourning, and the other is rejoicing and celebrating."

They made it halfway through the trip. "Joseph," Mary told him, "take me down from the donkey, because the one who's inside me is pushing to come out."

So he took her down from the donkey. "Where can I take you for some privacy?" he asked. "This place has no shelter."

Chapter 18: Time Stands Still

He found a cave nearby, brought her to it, stationed his sons with her, and went to look for a Hebrew midwife in the region of Bethlehem.

Now I, Joseph, was wandering but not wandering. I looked up to the dome of heaven and saw it standing still. I looked into the sky and was amazed to see that even the birds of heaven were still. I looked at the ground, and I saw a bowl lying there, and workers reclining around it. Their hands were in the bowl, and they were chewing but not chewing, and picking up food but not picking up food, and bringing it to their mouths but not bringing it to their mouths. Rather, they were all staring up.

I saw sheep being driven, but the sheep stood still. The shepherd lifted his hand to strike them, but his raised hand was frozen in place. I looked into the rushing river and saw young goats. Their mouths were in the water, but they weren't drinking.

All of a sudden, everything went back to normal.

Chapter 19: Jesus' Birth

And look! A woman was coming down from the mountain. She asked me, "Hey you, where are you going?"

I said, "I'm looking for a Hebrew midwife."

"Are you from Israel?"

"Yes."

"And who's the one giving birth in that cave?"

"My fiancé."

"So she's not your wife?"

"Mary was nurtured in the Lord's Temple," I replied, "and it was decided by lot that she would be my wife. She's not my wife yet, but she's conceived by the Holy Spirit."

"Really?" the midwife asked.

"Come and see," Joseph told her.

So the midwife went with him. They stood in front of the cave, and a bright cloud overshadowed it. "My soul is magnified today," the midwife said, "because my eyes have seen something wonderful. Salvation has been born to Israel!"

Immediately the cloud withdrew from the cave, and a light appeared, so bright that their eyes couldn't bear it. A little later, the light dimmed until an infant appeared. He went to the breast of his mother, Mary.

Then the midwife cried out. "How great today is for me," she exclaimed, "that I've seen this new miracle!"

Then the midwife went out of the cave, and Salome met her.

"Salome, Salome," she told her, "I have to describe a new sight to you. A virgin has given birth, which is against her nature!"

But Salome replied, "As the Lord my God lives, unless I examine her condition, I won't believe that the virgin has given birth."

Chapter 20: Salome's Examination

The midwife went in and said, "Mary, get ready, because you're about to experience a serious test."

And Salome examined her. Then Salome cried out. "I'm sorry," she cried, "because of my lawlessness and my unbelief! I've tested the living God, and look! My hand is on fire and falling off!"

So she dropped to her knees before the Lord. "God of my ancestors," she pleaded, "remember me, that I've descended from Abraham, Isaac, and Jacob. Don't make an example of me to the people of Israel, but give me back to the poor, because you know, Lord, that in your name I've healed people, and I've received my reward from you."

And look! An angel of the Lord appeared. "Salome, Salome," it told her, "the Lord of All has heard your prayer. Bring your hand to the child and lift him up, and you'll receive salvation and joy."

So Salome joyfully went to the child and lifted him up. "I bow to him," she said, "because a great king has been born to Israel." Immediately Salome was healed, and she left the cave justified.

And look! A voice said, "Salome, Salome, don't report the wonderful things you've seen until the child comes into Jerusalem."

Chapter 21: The Magi

And look! Joseph got ready to go out into Judea when a great commotion arose in Bethlehem of Judea, because magi came. "Where is the king of the Jews?" they asked. "Because we saw his star in the East and have come to bow to him."

When Herod heard this, he was disturbed. He sent officers to the magi, and sent for the chief priests and questioned them in his palace. "What's been written about the Christ?" he asked them. "Where will he be born?"

"In Bethlehem of Judea," they told him, "because that's what's written." So he let the chief priests go.

Then he questioned the magi. "What sign did you see about the one who's been born king?" he asked them.

The magi replied, "We saw an immense star shining among the other stars, dimming them so much that they weren't even visible. So we knew that a king had been born for Israel, and we came to bow to him."

"Go and search," Herod told them, "and if you find him, report to me so that I can come and bow to him, too."

So the magi left, and look! The star they had seen in the East led them until they came to the cave, and it stopped over the entrance of the cave. When they saw him with his mother Mary, the magi took gifts from their bags: gold, frankincense, and myrrh.

Then, having been warned by the angel not to go into Judea, they returned to their country by another way.

Chapter 22: The Slaughter of the Infants

When Herod saw that he had been tricked by the magi, he was furious. He sent out his assassins, telling them to kill all the infants two years old and younger.

Mary was afraid when she heard that the infants were being killed. She took her child, wrapped him in cloths, and put him in a manger for cows.

And when Elizabeth heard that they were looking for John, she took him up into the hills and looked around for somewhere to hide him, but there wasn't a hiding place. Then Elizabeth groaned. She pleaded, "Mountain of God, take a mother with a child," because Elizabeth was unable to climb any higher. The mountain immediately split in half and let her in, and a light shone through the mountain for her, because an angel of the Lord was with them, protecting them.

Chapter 23: The Murder of Zechariah

Herod specifically asked for John. He sent officers to Zechariah to ask him, "Where are you hiding your son?"

"I'm a minister of God," he told them, "and I sit in God's Temple. How should I know where my son is?"

So the officers went away and reported all these things to Herod. Herod was furious. "His son is about to be king over Israel!" he shouted.

So he sent his officers back to say, "Tell me the truth. Where's your son? You know that your life is in my hands."

And the officers went back and reported these things to him.

"I'll be a martyr of God if you shed my blood," Zechariah replied. "The Lord will receive my spirit, since you'll be spilling innocent blood at the entrance of the Lord's Temple."

Zechariah was murdered at about daybreak, but the people of Israel didn't know that he had been murdered.

Chapter 24: Mourning for Zechariah

And at the hour of greeting, the priests came, but Zechariah didn't meet them to bless them as usual. So the priests stood around for Zechariah, waiting to greet him with a blessing and to glorify the Most High God.

But when he didn't come, they were all afraid. One of them gathered the courage to go into the sanctuary and saw clotted blood beside the Lord's altar. "Zechariah has been murdered," a voice said, "and his blood won't be wiped away until his avenger comes!"

When he heard this, he was afraid, and he went and reported to the priests what he had seen and heard. Then they gathered their courage, went in, and saw what had taken place. The panels of the Temple cried out, and the priests ripped their clothes from top to bottom. They didn't find his corpse, but they did find that his blood had turned to stone. They were afraid, and they went out and reported to all the people that Zechariah had been murdered. When all the tribes of the people heard, they mourned him and wept three days and three nights.

After three days, the priests held a council about who should replace Zechariah. The lot fell to Simeon, because the Holy Spirit had told him that he wouldn't see death until he saw the Christ in the flesh.

Chapter 25: Conclusion

Now I, James, wrote this history in Jerusalem when there was a commotion over Herod's death. I went to the wilderness until the commotion in Jerusalem had died down. I was glorifying the Lord God, who gave me the wisdom to write this history.

Grace will be with all who fear the Lord. Amen.

3
Exploring the Infancy Gospel of Thomas

Originally known simply as "the Childhood Deeds of Jesus," this text later became known as the Infancy Gospel of Thomas (based on the identification of Thomas as the author in the prologue). Manuscripts of this Gospel have been preserved in Ethiopic, Georgian, Latin, Slavonic, Syriac, and a number of Greek manuscripts.[1]

Like the Infancy Gospel of James, the Infancy Gospel of Thomas, originally written in Greek in the second century, builds on earlier Scriptures and Gospels to tell a new story about Jesus. The author draws from not only the canonical New Testament Gospels (especially Luke and John), but the Gospel of Thomas as well. In addition, Infancy Thomas uses Genesis, Proverbs, and 1 Corinthians.[2] It picks up where Infancy James leaves off, narrating an incredible (and to contemporary ears, frankly weird) story about Jesus from ages five to twelve, concluding with a version of Luke's story of Jesus in the temple (cf. Luke 2:41-52).

This Gospel is very different from Infancy James, however. Whereas Infancy James is clearly respectful of Jews and Jewish institutions, Infancy Thomas builds on other Gospels' more crude caricatures of Jews.[3] In the beginning of the Gospel, Jesus is scolded for violating the Sabbath, and he responds with shocking callousness, just as an impulsive five-year-old might – if that five-year-old wielded divine power to strike down anyone who annoyed him.

This negative valuation of Judaism is also reflected in Jesus' conflicts with his teachers, whom he consistently outwits. The educational setting of these conflicts appears to be the synagogue;

the Mishnah specifies that Torah study should begin at age five.[4] Another strong indication that Jesus is portrayed in conflict with Rabbinic Judaism is suggested by the name of his first teacher, Zacchaeus. Jacob Neusner has explored the connection between this Zacchaeus and an actual first-century Rabbi. He writes:

> One is struck by the fact that the name Zaccheus is known to have been borne by a contemporary of Jesus, Rabban Yohanan ben Zakkai [Zacchaeus], who actually lived in Galilee ca. 20-40 C.E. ... I suggest that the story [of Infancy Thomas 6 and 7] arose, in its original form, in the Jewish-Christian community in Galilee after 70 C.E., and that it was intended to liberate the community from the authority of R. Yohanan ben Zakkai's academy at Yavneh.[5]

Whereas Jesus easily outwits Zacchaeus, his second teacher is much less fortunate; Jesus actually strikes him dead in chapter 14. Such impulsive behavior is a recurring theme in Infancy Thomas. It arguably reflects 1 Corinthians 13:11,[6] in which Paul writes that:

> When I was a child,
> I spoke like a child,
> thought like a child,
> reasoned like a child.
> Now that I've grown up,
> I've put away childish things (DFV).

Especially given the official Christian doctrine that Jesus was "truly human," wouldn't one expect Jesus, as a human child, to act impulsively? What would it be like for Jesus, as fully human, to grow from childish immaturity into responsible adulthood? This appears to be what Infancy Thomas explores.

The fact that Infancy Thomas portrays Jesus' immaturity through age twelve is no accident. Samuel Zinner plausibly suggests that the author was familiar with traditional Jewish teaching that "children are not really accountable for objectively bad deeds"[7] (even though that tradition obviously didn't contemplate murder).[8]

It's as if this Gospel illustrates in vivid detail what Luke 2:52 might look like in actual practice: "Jesus grew in wisdom and stature" (DFV). That Jesus experiences gradual maturity during this time is evident by the fact that he later rescinds his curses. In chapter 8, he brings back to life the children he struck down in chapters 3 and 4, and in chapter 15, he brings back to life the teacher he killed in the previous chapter.

Considering the social context of this Gospel and of ancient attitudes toward children, as well as drawing several inferences throughout the text, Reidar Aasgaard builds a strong argument that Infancy Thomas teaches a fully "orthodox" Christology,[9] that "Jesus emerges in the Christology of [Infancy Thomas] as a combination of a divine Christ and a true-to-life child."[10] Though his argument is plausible, others have discerned little or no Christology proper at all in this Gospel. Interestingly, Jesus is never explicitly described as "Lord" or "Christ" except in the prologue, which was only later added to the Gospel.[11] In chapter 9, when he's called *kyrios* in the Greek, it's most likely in the sense of "sir" rather than "Lord."[12] And references to Jesus "saving souls" in chapters 10 and 18 are likely descriptions of this-worldly healings, as in chapters 8, 15, and 16.

Christology may not be a central feature of Infancy Thomas, but that doesn't mean it has no theological reflection about Jesus. The teacher Zacchaeus in this Gospel wonders about Jesus' identity: "this child is a great thing – whether a god or an angel or whatever else – I don't know" (chapter 7).

Zinner has argued persuasively that both 1 Corinthians 13 and the poetic theological language about Wisdom ("Sophiology") in ancient Jewish literature have shaped this Gospel's portrayal of Jesus. He writes that Infancy Thomas:

> thus shares a main background of the Johannine Christology, namely, the Sophiology of Proverbs 8 and related texts (e.g., Sirach 24, Baruch 3-4). [Infancy Thomas] portrays Jesus as an

earthly manifestation of pre-existent Lady Wisdom who plays among humans (Proverbs 8), and who in human form acts childishly at first, later maturing into an adult (cf. 1 Corinthians 13). Proverbs 8 and 1 Corinthians 13 have therefore been creatively combined in order to form [Infancy Thomas'] model for understanding Jesus.[13]

In its portrayal of Jesus as Wisdom incarnate, it appears that Infancy Thomas chapter 6 derives from Proverbs 8:22 the idea that Jesus was a created being, which may not have been a controversial idea at the time (even though it wouldn't be consistent with the doctrine of later Church Councils). However, the phrase in question is admittedly unclear in the Greek, and other translators have rendered it in different ways (cf. the Text Note on Chapter 6 in Appendix B).

Scholars have noted how Infancy Thomas chapter 2 recalls the language of the creation story in Genesis. The child Jesus orders the waters (cf. Gen. 1:1, 6-10) and creates living beings out of clay (cf. Gen. 2:7).[14] Infancy Thomas draws on the description of Lady Wisdom in Proverbs 8 and similar texts, together with John 1, to shape its portrayal of Jesus.

Despite its negative portrayal of Jews, Infancy Thomas not only drew from the well of Jewish tradition, it may have influenced it as well, particularly in the story of the alphabet in chapter 6. Jesus' mystical knowledge of the alphabet in this text may have influenced later Jewish letter mysticism.[15]

By shaping earlier traditions in the context of rural life in late antiquity, Infancy Thomas is not simply, as some have initially thought, a bizarre tale with little value for understanding the development of the Jesus movement. On the contrary, if we take the time to consider it more closely, we may find that it can provide a unique window into how some of Jesus' middle- to low-class followers sought to define their identity over against other social groups – including how they sought to legitimize their faith and practice at the expense of Jews.

About This Translation

Infancy Thomas exists in a variety of manuscripts. The new translation which follows is based on the earliest Greek text, which doesn't contain chapters 17 or 18. Consequently, those chapters have been translated from later manuscripts. In the earliest Greek copy, chapter 10 is actually placed where chapters 17 and 18 appear in later versions, but has been repositioned here to accommodate the additions of chapters 17 and 18 and to track with better-known versions and translations.

For more information about the manuscript tradition, see the introductory comments to the more literal translation in Appendix B.

Parentheses in the translation denote editorial insertions. Daggers denote an editorial revision, angled brackets denote an unintelligible word, and square brackets denote a gap in the text.

4
The Infancy Gospel of Thomas
A New Translation

Chapter 1: Prologue

I, Thomas the Israelite, thought I needed to reveal to all the Gentile brothers (and sisters) everything our Lord Jesus Christ did in the village of Nazareth, after he was born in our region of Bethlehem. This is how it begins:

Chapter 2: Jesus Makes Sparrows

The child Jesus was five years old. After it rained, he was playing at the ford of a flowing stream. Stirring up the dirty waters, he collected them into pools. He made them clean and pure just by his word – not by doing anything.

Then, taking soft clay from the mud, he formed twelve sparrows. It was the Sabbath when he did this, and many children were with him.

A certain Jew saw the child Jesus with the other children doing all this. He went to his father Joseph and accused the child Jesus.

"He made clay on the Sabbath, which isn't right," he said, "and he formed twelve sparrows."

Joseph went and scolded (Jesus). "Why are you doing these things on the Sabbath?" he asked.

But Jesus clapped his hands, ordering the birds in front of everyone. "Fly away like living beings!" he shouted. The sparrows squawked and flew away.

⁵ When he saw this, the Pharisee was amazed, and he reported it to all his friends.

Chapter 3: Jesus Curses Annas' Son

The son of Annas the high priest asked (Jesus), "Why are you doing such a thing on the Sabbath?" Taking a willow twig, he destroyed the pools and drained the water which Jesus had gathered, and he dried them up.

When he saw what had happened, Jesus told him, "Your fruit (will have) no root, and your shoot will be withered like a scorched branch in a violent wind!"

That child withered away immediately.

Chapter 4: Jesus Curses a Careless Child

As (Jesus) was leaving there with his father Joseph, someone running by struck his shoulder. "May you be cursed because of your leader!" Jesus told him.

He died immediately.

The people who saw this cried out. "Where was this child born, that what he says comes true?"

When the parents of the dead child saw what had happened, they blamed his father Joseph. "Wherever your child is from, you can't live with us in this village. If you want to be here, teach him to bless and not to curse, because our child has been taken from us."

Chapter 5: Joseph Confronts Jesus

Joseph said to Jesus, "Why do you say such things? They suffer and hate us!"

The child told Joseph, "Since you know wise words, you're not ignorant of where they came from. They were spoken about a five-year-old.† They won't be raised, and these people will receive their punishment."

Those accusing him were blinded immediately.

Joseph grabbed (Jesus') ear and pulled hard.

Jesus told him, "It's enough for you seek and find me, and not, beyond that, to scourge me in ignorance. You haven't clearly seen why I'm yours. Look! I've been subdued before you."

Chapter 6: First Teacher, Zacchaeus

A teacher named Zacchaeus (was) standing (there), very amazed to hear Jesus saying these things to his father Joseph.

He told Joseph, "Come, give him (to me), Brother, so that he may be taught letters, so that he may learn all things, learn to love those his own age, honor old age, and respect elders, so that he may acquire a yearning to be around children, teaching them in return."

"And who can control this child and teach him?" Joseph asked the teacher. "Don't think of him as a small person, Brother."

"Give him to me, Brother," said the teacher, "and don't let him concern you."

Then the child Jesus looked at them and gave this speech to the teacher: "Being a teacher comes naturally to you, but you're a stranger to the name, because I'm outside of you and I'm within you on account of the nobility of my birth in the flesh. But you, a lawyer, don't know the law."

And to Joseph he said, "When you were born, I existed, standing beside you so that as a father you may be taught something by me which no one else knows or can teach. And you will bear the name of salvation."

The Jews cried out and said, "Oh new and incredible wonder! The child is perhaps five years old, and oh, what words he says! We've never known such words. No one – neither a lawyer nor a Pharisee – has ever spoken like this child."

"Why are you amazed?" the child asked. "Or rather, why don't you believe the things I've said to you? The truth is that I was created before this world, and I know accurately when you were born, and your ancestors, and their ancestors."

Everyone who heard this was speechless, no longer able to talk to him. He went up to them and skipped around. "I was just playing with you," he said, "because I know you're small-minded, and amazed with small things."

Now when they seemed comforted by the child's encouragement, the teacher told his father, "Come, bring him into the school. I'll teach him letters."

So Joseph took him by the hand and led him to the school. The teacher flattered him and brought him inside. Then Zacchaeus wrote the alphabet for him and started teaching him, repeating the same letter frequently. But the child didn't say anything.

The teacher became irritated and struck him on the head.

Then the child became irritated. "I want to teach you rather than be taught by you," he said, "since I know the letters you're teaching better than you do. To me these things are like a noisy gong or a clanging cymbal that don't bring out the sound, glory, or power of understanding."

When the child's anger ceased, he very skillfully recited all the letters by himself, from the alpha to the omega. He looked straight at the teacher. "If you don't know the nature of the alpha," he asked, "how can you teach someone else the beta? Hypocrite! If you know, first teach me the alpha, and then I will trust you to talk about the beta." Then he began to teach the teacher about the first element. And he couldn't say anything to him.

While many listened, he told the teacher, "Listen, Teacher, and understand the arrangement of the first letter. Now, notice how it has sharp lines and a middle stroke, which you see pointing, standing with legs apart, coming together, going out, dragging behind, lifting up, dancing around, <...>, in triple rhythm, two-cornered, of the same form, of the same thickness, of the same family, raised, balanced, isometric, of equal proportions. These are the lines of the alpha."

Chapter 7: Zacchaeus' Lament

When the teacher heard Jesus express such good familiarity (and) talk about the lines of the first letter, he was baffled by such teaching and Jesus' defense.

"I'm so sad!" the teacher said. "I'm so sad! I've been baffled and am miserable. I've brought shame on myself by taking on this child.

"Take (him) away from me, Brother, because I can't bear his gaze or the clarity of his word. This child is simply out of this world. He can even tame fire! Maybe this child even existed before the creation of the world. What kind of womb bore him? What kind of mother raised him? I don't know. I'm so sad, Brother! He stupefies me. My mind can't follow him. I've deceived myself, thrice-unhappy as I am. I thought to gain a disciple, but ended up having a teacher.

"Friends, I ponder my shame, old man that I am, that I've been defeated by a child. I should be cast out and die, or flee this village because of this child. I can't be seen among all you anymore, especially those of you who saw me defeated by a very small child. But what can I say or tell anyone about the lines of the first letter? The truth is I don't know, friends, because I don't understand either the beginning or the end!

"Therefore, Brother Joseph, lead him away with salvation to your house, because this child is a great thing – whether a god or an angel or whatever else – I don't know."

Chapter 8: Jesus' Response

The child Jesus laughed. "Now may the barren bear fruit, the blind see, and the foolish in heart find understanding," he said. "I'm here from above, so I may rescue those below and call them up, just as the one who sent me to you has ordered me."

All who had fallen under his curse were saved immediately. No one dared to provoke him from then on.

Chapter 9: Jesus Raises Zeno

Many days later, Jesus was playing with other children on someone's upper story roof. But one of the children fell and died. The other children saw this and went home. They left Jesus alone.

Then the parents of the dead child came and accused Jesus. "You pushed down our child!" they said.

But Jesus said, "I didn't push him down."

As they were raging and shouting, Jesus jumped down from the roof. He stood beside the body and cried out in a loud voice, "Zeno, Zeno" – because that was (the child's) name – "Rise and say whether or not I pushed you down."

He rose and said, "No, sir."

When they saw it, (the parents) were amazed.

Jesus told him, "Fall asleep!"

Then the parents of the child praised God and worshipped the child Jesus.

Chapter 10: Jesus Heals a Woodcutter

Then a certain young man was splitting wood into equal pieces. But he split the bottom of his foot, bled out, and died.

A commotion arose, and Jesus ran there. Forcing his way through the crowd, he seized the stricken foot. It healed immediately. Then he told the young man, "Go, split your wood."

When the crowds saw this, they were amazed. "For he saved many souls from death," they said, "and he will continue to save all the days of his life."

Chapter 11: Jesus Carries Water in his Cloak

When the child Jesus was about seven years old, his mother Mary sent him to draw water. But the water cistern was crowded, and the pitcher was struck and broke.

But Jesus spread out the cloak he was wearing, filled it with water, and carried it to his mother. When Mary saw what miracle Jesus had done, she kissed him. "Lord, my God," she prayed, "bless our child." They were afraid that someone might cast a spell on him.

Chapter 12: Miracle of the Harvest

When it was time to sow, Joseph sowed seeds, and the child Jesus sowed one measure of wheat.

His father reaped a hundred great measures, and he gave graciously to the poor and the orphans. But Joseph took from Jesus' seeds.

Chapter 13: Miracle of the Bed

Now (Jesus) was about eight years old. His father was a carpenter who made ploughs and yokes. He took a bed from a certain rich man so that he might make it very great and suitable. But one of the beams, called the (...), was shorter; it wasn't the (right) length. Joseph was upset; he didn't know what to do.

The child came to his father. "Put down the two boards," he said, "and line them up on your end."

So Joseph did what he said. The child Jesus stood at the other end, seized the short board, and stretched it, making it equal with the other board.

Then he said to his father, "Don't be upset, but make whatever you want to."

Joseph embraced and kissed him. "Blessed am I," he said, "that God gave this child to me."

Chapter 14: Second Teacher

When Joseph saw (Jesus') wisdom and understanding, he didn't want him to be illiterate, but signed him up with another teacher.

The teacher wrote the alphabet for (Jesus). "Say alpha," he instructed.

"First you tell me what the beta is," the child replied, "and I'll tell you what the alpha is."

Irritated, the teacher struck him. Jesus cursed him, and the teacher fell down and died.

Then the child went home to his parents. Joseph called (Jesus') mother and ordered her not to let (Jesus) out of the house so that anyone provoking him wouldn't die.

Chapter 15: Third Teacher

After some time, another teacher told (Jesus') father Joseph, "Come, Brother, give him to me in the school so that with flattery I can teach him letters."

Joseph told him, "If you have the courage, Brother, take him with salvation."

So the teacher took the child by the hand and led him away with much fear and concern. The child was glad to go.

Entering the school, (Jesus) found a book lying on the lectern. He picked it up, but he didn't read what it said, because it wasn't from God's law. Instead, he started talking, and he said things that were so impressive that the teacher seated across from him listened very gladly and encouraged him to talk more. The crowd standing there was amazed by his holy words.

Joseph ran quickly to the school, suspecting that this teacher was no longer inexperienced and had suffered. But the teacher told Joseph, "Just so you know, Brother, I did indeed take your child as a disciple, but he's full of much grace and wisdom. So, Brother, lead him away with salvation into your house."

(Jesus) told the teacher, "Since you spoke and testified correctly, the (teacher who was) struck down will also be saved because of you." So that teacher also was saved immediately. Taking the child, (Joseph) led (Jesus) home.

Chapter 16: Jesus Heals James' Snakebite

James went into the grove to tie up sticks so that they might make bread. Jesus went with him too. As they were gathering the sticks, a terrible snake bit James' hand.

As he was sprawled out and dying, the child Jesus ran to James and blew on the bite. The bite was healed immediately. The beast was destroyed, and James was saved.

Chapter 17: Jesus Heals a Baby

After these things, in Joseph's neighborhood a certain baby fell sick and died. His mother wept intensely.

But when Jesus heard that there was great grief and commotion, he ran quickly. He found the child dead and touched his chest. "I tell you, baby," he said, "don't die, but live, and be with your mother."

(The baby) looked up immediately and laughed. Then (Jesus) said to the mother, "Pick up your child, nurse him, and remember me."

The crowd standing there was amazed. "The truth is," they said, "that this child (Jesus) is either a god or an angel, because everything he says comes true!"

Then Jesus went away again to play with the (other) children.

Chapter 18: Jesus Heals a Builder

Some time later, a building was being constructed. There was a great commotion, and Jesus got up and went there.

Seeing a man lying dead, (Jesus) seized (the man's) hand. "I tell you, man," he said, "rise and do your work." Then (the man) rose immediately and worshipped him.

When the crowds saw this, they were amazed. "For he saved many souls from death," they said, "and he will continue to save all the days of his life."

Chapter 19: Jesus in the Temple

When Jesus was twelve years old, his parents went, as usual, to Jerusalem for the festival of the Passover. But when they returned, Jesus stayed behind in Jerusalem without his parents' knowledge.

Assuming him to be in the traveling company, they went a day's journey and then searched for him among their known relatives. When they didn't find him, they returned to Jerusalem and searched for him there.

After three days, they found him in the temple sitting in the middle of the teachers, listening to them and questioning them. Those listening to him were surprised at how he questioned the elders and explained the main points of the law and the riddles and parables of the prophets.

"Child, what have you done to us?" his mother asked. "Look, we've been hurt and upset searching for you."

"Why were you looking for me?" Jesus asked. "Didn't you know that I need to be in my Father's house?"

The scribes and the Pharisees asked Mary, "You're the mother of this child?"

"I am," she said.

"Blessed are you," they told her, "that the Lord God has blessed the fruit of your womb, because we've never seen such wisdom of praise and glory of virtue."

Then Jesus stood up and followed his mother from there, and was obedient to his parents. She treasured all these things, pondering them in her heart.

And Jesus advanced in wisdom and maturity and grace before God and humans. To whom be the [glory ...].

Appendix A:
A Public Domain Version of
the Infancy Gospel of James

This translation has been committed to the public domain. It may be freely copied and used, in whole or in part, changed or unchanged, for any purpose.

There are over 140 known manuscripts containing the Greek text of the Infancy Gospel of James (with varying titles). Scholars have divided the manuscripts into five families. The Papyrus Bodmer V, which dates to the late third or early fourth century, was unknown at the time of von Tischendorf's nineteenth-century transcript, which was the basis for many earlier translations.

This translation is principally based on the standard 1961 critical text of Émile de Strycker (which incorporated the Bodmer Papyrus), though most of the paragraph breaks here follow the more recent transcript of Ronald Hock. This translation also follows the traditional chapter divisions and sections.

Symbols

(   ) Editorial insertion

Chapter 1: Joachim's Plight

(1) In the histories of the twelve tribes of Israel, Joachim was a very rich man. And he doubled the gifts he offered to the Lord, saying to himself, "One is from my surplus for all the people, and the other is to the Lord God for forgiveness, to atone for me."

(2) Now the great day of the Lord was approaching, and the people of Israel were offering their gifts. But Reubel stood before him and said, "It's not right for you to offer your gifts first, since you haven't had a child in Israel."

(3) And Joachim was very grieved and went to the (history) of the twelve tribes of the people, saying to himself, "I'll look in the (history) of the twelve tribes of Israel to see whether I'm the only one who hasn't had a child in Israel." And he searched, and found that all the just people in Israel had raised children. And he remembered that in the last days of the patriarch Abraham, the Lord God gave him a son, Isaac.

(4) And Joachim was very grieved, and didn't go to his wife, but gave himself to the wilderness and pitched his tent there. And Joachim fasted forty days and forty nights, saying to himself, "I won't go down for food or drink until the Lord my God considers me. Prayer will be my food and drink."

Chapter 2: Anna's Plight

(1) Now his wife, Anna, mourned and lamented for two reasons. She said, "I lament that I'm a widow and that I don't have a child."

(2) Now the great day of the Lord was approaching, and her servant Juthine said to her, "How long are you going to humiliate your soul? Look, the great day of the Lord has approached, and it's not right for you to grieve. But take this headband which the leader of the workplace gave me. It's not right for me to wear it, since I'm your servant, and it has a royal mark."

(3) And Anna said, "Get away from me! I won't do this. The Lord God has greatly humiliated me. Maybe a trickster gave this to you, and you've come to get me to share in your sin."

And Juthine the servant said, "Why should I curse you, since you haven't heard my voice? The Lord God has made your womb infertile, to give you no fruit in Israel."

(4) And Anna was very grieved, and removed her garment of mourning, washed her head, and put on her wedding garment.

And at about the ninth hour she went down into her garden to walk around. She saw a laurel tree and sat down under it. And after resting, she petitioned the Lord. She said, "God of my ancestors, bless me and hear my prayer, as you blessed our mother Sarah and gave her a son, Isaac."

Chapter 3: Anna's Lament

(1) Anna looked intently to heaven and saw a nest of sparrows in the laurel tree. And Anna lamented, saying to herself,

"Woe is me! Who gave birth to me? What womb bore me? I was born as a curse before the people of Israel and have been despised; they've mocked me and banished me from the Temple of the Lord my God.

(2) "Woe is me! What am I like? I'm not like the birds of heaven, because even the birds of heaven are fruitful before you, Lord.

"Woe is me! What am I like? I'm not like the animals, because even the animals are fruitful before you, Lord.

"Woe is me! What am I like? I'm not like the wild beasts of the earth, because even the wild beasts of the earth are fruitful before you, Lord.

(3) "Woe is me! What am I like? I'm not like these waters, because even these waters are serene yet churn, and their fish bless you, Lord.

"Woe is me! What am I like? I'm not like this earth, because the earth produces her fruits when it's time and blesses you, Lord."

Chapter 4: The Lord's Promise

(1) And look! An angel of the Lord stood nearby, saying to her, "Anna, Anna, the Lord has heard your prayer. You'll conceive and give birth, and your offspring will be spoken of through the whole world."

And Anna said, "As the Lord God lives, whether I give birth to a boy or a girl, I'll bring it as a gift to the Lord my God, and it will minister to him all the days of its life."

(2) And look! Two angels came, saying to her, "Look, Joachim, your husband, is coming with his flocks." For an angel of the Lord had gone down to Joachim, saying, "Joachim, Joachim, the Lord God has heard your prayer. Go down from here. Look, your wife, Anna, has conceived in her womb."

(3) And immediately Joachim went down and called the shepherds, saying to them, "Bring here to me ten lambs without spot or blemish, and the ten lambs will be for the Lord God. And bring me twelve tender calves for the priests and the elders. And a hundred male goats for all the people."

(4) And look! Joachim came with his flocks, and Anna stood at the gate. And she saw Joachim coming with his flocks, and immediately ran and flung herself around his neck, saying, "Now I know that the Lord God has greatly blessed me. For look! The widow is no longer a widow, and look! The one without a child in her womb has conceived."

And Joachim rested for the first day in his house.

Chapter 5: Mary's Birth

(1) And the next day, he was offering his gifts, saying to himself, "If the Lord God is reconciled to me, the plate worn by the priest will make it clear to me." And Joachim offered his gifts and paid attention to the priest's plate as he went up to the altar of the Lord. And he didn't see sin in it. And Joachim said, "Now I know that the Lord God has been reconciled to me and has sent

all my sins away from me." And he went down from the Temple of the Lord justified and went into his house.

(2) And about six months were completed, and in the seventh month she gave birth. And Anna said to her midwife, "What is it?"

And the midwife said, "It's a girl!"

And Anna said, "My soul is magnified this day!" And she laid down her child.

And when her days were completed, Anna cleansed her menstrual flow. And she gave her breast to the child, and gave her the name Mary.

Chapter 6: Mary's First Year

(1) And day by day, the child grew stronger. When she was six months old, her mother stood her on the ground to test whether she could stand. And walking seven steps, she came to her mother's breast, and her mother caught her up, saying, "As the Lord my God lives, you won't walk on this ground again until I bring you into the Temple of the Lord."

And she made a sanctuary in her bedroom and didn't allow anything sacrilegious or impure to pass through it. And she called the pure daughters of the Hebrews, and they played with her.

(2) And when the child grew to be a year old, Joachim made a great feast, and called the chief priests, and the priests, and the scribes, and the elders, and all the people of Israel. And Joachim brought the child to the priests, and they blessed her, saying, "God of our ancestors, bless this child and give her a name that'll be spoken forever among all generations."

And all the people said, "So be it. Amen!"

And they brought her to the chief priests, and they blessed her, saying, "Most High God, look upon this child, and bless her with a final blessing which can't be surpassed."

(3) And her mother took her up to the sanctuary of her bedroom and gave her breast to the child. And Anna made a song to the Lord God, saying:

"I'll sing a holy song to the Lord my God, because God has visited me, and has removed the criticism of my enemies.

"And the Lord God has given me the fruit of God's justice, singular yet manifold before God.

"Who will report to Reubel's people that Anna nurses a child? 'Listen, listen, twelve tribes of Israel: Anna nurses a child!'"

And Anna rested in the sanctuary of her bedroom. And she went and ministered to them. When dinner was finished, they went down rejoicing and glorifying the God of Israel.

Chapter 7: Mary Goes to the Temple

(1) And she cared for her child through the months. When she was two years old, Joachim said, "Let's take her to the Temple of the Lord, so that we may keep the promise we made, so that the Lord won't be angry with us and find our gift unacceptable."
But Anna said, "Let's wait until her third year, so that she won't seek her father or mother."
And Joachim said, "Let's wait."
(2) And the child became three years old, and Joachim said, "Let's call the pure daughters of the Hebrews. And let them take their lamps, and let them be lit, so that the child won't turn back, and her heart won't be drawn away from the Temple of the Lord." And they did so until they went up to the Temple of the Lord.
And the priest welcomed her, kissed her, and said, "The Lord God has magnified your name among all the generations. Through you, the Lord will reveal his redemption of the people of Israel in the last days."
(3) And he sat her down on the third step of the altar, and the Lord God poured grace upon her. And she danced on her feet, and all the house of Israel loved her.

Chapter 8: Mary Turns Twelve

(1) And her parents went down, marveling and praising and glorifying the Lord God that the child hadn't turned back. And Mary was in the Temple of the Lord. She was nurtured like a dove, and received food from the hand of an angel.

(2) And when she became twelve years old, there was a council of the priests, saying, "Look, Mary has been in the Temple of the Lord twelve years. What should we do about her so that she won't pollute the sanctuary of the Lord our God?" And they said to the chief priest, "You stand at the altar of the Lord. Go in and pray about her, and if the Lord God reveals anything to you, we'll do it."

(3) And the chief priest went in, taking the robe with twelve bells into the Holy of Holies, and prayed about her. And look! An angel of the Lord stood nearby, saying, "Zechariah, Zechariah, go out and assemble the widowers of the people, and let them each bear a staff. And whomever the Lord God points out with a sign, she'll be his wife."

And the heralds went down through the whole surrounding area of Judea, and sounded the trumpet of the Lord. And look! All the men rushed in.

Chapter 9: Joseph Protects Mary

(1) And Joseph threw down his axe, and went to their meeting. And when they had all gathered, they went to the priest with their staffs. And having taken all their staffs, he went into the Temple and prayed. And when he had finished the prayer, he took the staffs, went out, and gave them back. But there wasn't a sign among them. And Joseph took his staff last, and look! A dove went from the staff, and flew upon Joseph's head. And the priest said to Joseph, "You've been chosen to welcome the virgin of the Lord into your own care."

(2) But Joseph refused, saying, "I have sons and am an old man, but she's young. I won't be a laughingstock among the people of Israel."

And the priest said, "Joseph, fear the Lord your God, and remember what God did to Dathan, Abiron, and Kore; how the earth opened and swallowed them all because of their rebellion. And now fear, Joseph, so that these things won't happen in your house."

(3) And being afraid, Joseph welcomed her into his care, and said to her, "Mary, I've taken you from the Temple of the Lord, and now I bring you to my house. I'm going away to build houses, but I'll come back to you. The Lord will protect you."

Chapter 10: The Veil of the Temple

(1) And there was a council of the priests, saying, "Let's make a veil for the Temple of the Lord."

And the priest said, "Call the pure virgins from the tribe of David to me." And the officers went out and searched and found seven. And the priest remembered that the child Mary was from the tribe of David and pure before God. And the officers went out and brought her.

(2) And they brought them into the Temple of the Lord, and the priest said, "Cast lots for me to see who will spin the gold and the white and the linen and the silk and the violet and the scarlet and the true purple."

And the lot for the true purple and scarlet fell to Mary. And she took them into her house. This was the time that Zechariah fell silent, and Samuel took his place until Zechariah could speak. And Mary took the scarlet and was spinning it.

Chapter 11: The Annunciation

(1) And she took the pitcher and went to fill it with water, and look! A voice was saying to her, "Rejoice, blessed one! The Lord is with you. Blessed are you among women."

And Mary looked around to the right and the left, to see where the voice might be coming from. And she became terrified and went into her house. And setting down the pitcher, she took up the purple and sat upon her throne and spun the purple.

(2) And look! An angel of the Lord stood before her, saying, "Don't fear, Mary, because you've found grace before the Lord of All. You'll conceive from God's word."

And hearing this, Mary questioned herself, saying, "Will I conceive from the Lord, the living God, and give birth like all women give birth?"

(3) And the angel of the Lord said to her, "Not like that, Mary, because the power of God will overshadow you, so the holy one who will be born from you will be called the Son of the Most High. And you'll call his name Jesus, because he'll save his people from their sins.

And Mary said, "Look, I'm the servant of the Lord. May it be to me according to your word."

Chapter 12: Mary Visits Elizabeth

(1) And she made the purple and the scarlet, and she took it to the priest. And taking it, the priest blessed her and said, "Mary, the Lord God has magnified your name, and you'll be blessed among all the generations of the earth."

(2) And Mary rejoiced and went to her cousin Elizabeth. And she knocked at the door. And Elizabeth heard, flung down the scarlet, and rushed to the door. And she opened it and blessed her and said, "How is it that the mother of my Lord should come to me? Because look, the one in me leaped and blessed you!"

But Mary forgot the mysteries which Gabriel the angel had told her. And she looked intently into heaven and said, "Lord, who am I, that all the women of the earth will bless me?"

(3) And she spent three months with Elizabeth. And day by day, her womb grew larger, and Mary was afraid. She went to her house and hid herself from the people of Israel. She was sixteen years old when these mysteries happened to her.

Chapter 13: Joseph Questions Mary

(1) And she was in her sixth month. And look! Joseph came from his building, and came into the house, and found her pregnant. And he struck his face and flung himself on the ground in sackcloth and wept bitterly, saying, "How can I look to the Lord God? What prayer can I say about this young girl, since I took her as a virgin from the Temple of the Lord God and didn't protect her? Who has set this trap for me? Who has done this evil thing in my house? Who has defiled the virgin? Aren't I reliving the story of Adam? For as Adam was glorifying in the hour of prayer, the serpent came, found Eve alone, and deceived her, and now it's happened to me!"

(2) And Joseph stood from the sackcloth and called her and said to her, "God cared for you. Why have you done this? You've forgotten the Lord your God. Why have you humiliated your soul? You were nourished in the Holy of Holies and received food from the hand of an angel!"

(3) And she wept bitterly, saying, "I'm pure, and I haven't known a man!"

And Joseph said to her, "Where then did this thing in your womb come from?"

And she said, "As the Lord my God lives, I don't know where it came from!"

Chapter 14: Joseph's Dream

(1) And Joseph was very afraid and kept quiet about her, considering what to do about her. And Joseph said, "If I hide her sin, I'll be found resisting the law of the Lord, but if I reveal her to the people of Israel, I'm afraid that what's inside her might be angelic, and I'll be found handing over innocent blood to the judgment of death. So what will I do about her? I'll secretly set her free from me."

And night overtook him. (2) And look! An angel of the Lord appeared to him in a dream, saying, "Don't fear this child, for the one in her is from the Holy Spirit. And she'll give birth to a son, and you'll call his name 'Jesus,' because he'll save his people from their sins."

And Joseph arose from his sleep and glorified the God of Israel, who had given grace to him. And he protected her.

Chapter 15: The Chief Priest Questions Mary and Joseph

(1) And Annas the scribe came to him and said to him, "Joseph, why haven't you appeared among our traveling group?"

And he said to him, "Because I was weary from the trip and rested the first day back."

And Annas turned and saw Mary pregnant.

(2) And he quickly went to the priest and said to him, "Joseph, about whom you bore witness, has acted very lawlessly."

And the priest said, "What's this?"

And he said, "The virgin that Joseph took from the Temple of the Lord, he's defiled her and has stolen her wedding and hasn't revealed it to the people of Israel."

And in response the priest said, "Has Joseph done this?"

And Annas the scribe said to him, "Send officers, and you'll find the virgin pregnant."

And the officers went and found her just as he said. And they led her together with Joseph to the court.

(3) And the chief priest said to her, "Mary, why have you done this? Why have you humiliated your soul and forgotten the Lord your God? You were raised in the Holy of Holies, and received food from the hand of an angel, and you heard its hymns and danced before it. What is this that you've done?"

And she wept bitterly, saying, "As the Lord God lives, I'm pure before God, and I haven't known a man!"

(4) And the priest said, "Joseph, what is this that you've done?"

And Joseph said, "As the Lord my God lives, and the witness of God's truth, I'm pure toward her."

And the priest said, "Don't bear false witness, but tell the truth. You stole her wedding and didn't reveal it to the people of Israel, and you haven't bowed your head under the mighty hand that should bless your offspring."

And Joseph fell silent.

Chapter 16: The Test

(1) And the priest said, "Return the virgin you took from the Temple of the Lord."

And Joseph was tearful.

And the chief priest said, "I'll give you the water of the Lord's rebuke to drink, and it'll reveal your sin in your eyes."

(2) And taking (the water), the priest gave it to Joseph and sent him into the wilderness. And Joseph returned unharmed.

And he gave it to Mary and sent her into the wilderness. And she returned unharmed.

And all the people were amazed that their sin wasn't revealed.

(3) And the priest said, "If the Lord God hasn't revealed your sin to you, neither do I judge you." And he set them free.

And Joseph took Mary and went to his house, rejoicing and glorifying the God of Israel.

Chapter 17: The Census

(1) Now an order went out from Augustus the king to register how many people were in Bethlehem of Judea.

And Joseph said, "I'll register my sons. But what should I do about this child? How will I register her? As my wife? I'm ashamed. As my daughter? But the people of Israel know she's not my daughter. This is the day of the Lord; I'll do whatever the Lord wants."

(2) And he saddled the donkey, and sat her on it, and his son led it, and Samuel followed.

And as they neared the third mile, Joseph turned and saw that she was sad. And he was saying, "Likely the one inside her is troubling her."

And again Joseph turned and saw her laughing, and he said to her, "Mary, why are you like this, that I see your face laughing at one time, but then sad?"

And she said to him, "It's because I see two people in my eyes. One is crying and mourning, and one is rejoicing and exulting."

(3) And they came to the middle of the journey, and Mary said to him, "Joseph, take me down from the donkey, because the one who's inside me is pushing to come out."

And he took her down from the donkey and said to her, "Where will I take you and shelter you in your awkwardness? This place is a wilderness."

Chapter 18: Time Stands Still

(1) And he found a cave there, brought her to it, and stationed his sons with her and went to look for a Hebrew midwife in the region of Bethlehem.

(2) Now I, Joseph, was wandering but not wandering. And I looked up to the dome of heaven and saw it standing still, and into the sky, and I was astonished to see that even the birds of heaven were still. And I looked at the ground and saw a bowl lying there, and workers reclining, and their hands were in the bowl, and they were chewing but not chewing, and they were picking up food but not picking up food, and they were bringing it to their mouths but not bringing it to their mouths. Rather, all their faces were looking up.

And I saw sheep being driven, but the sheep stood still. And the shepherd lifted his hand to strike them, but his hand was raised. And I looked into the torrent of the river and saw young goats, and their mouths were in the water but not drinking.

And suddenly, everything resumed its course.

Chapter 19: Jesus' Birth

(1) And look! A woman was coming down from the mountain, and she said to me, "Man, where are you going?"

And I said, "I'm seeking a Hebrew midwife."

And in reply she said to me, "Are you from Israel?"

And I said to her, "Yes."

Then she said, "And who's the one giving birth in the cave?"

And I said, "My betrothed."

And she said to me, "She's not your wife?"

And I said to her, "Mary was nurtured in the Temple of the Lord, and it was decided by lot that she would be my wife, yet she's not my wife; but she's conceived from the Holy Spirit."

And the midwife said, "Really?"

And Joseph said to her, "Come and see."

And the midwife went with him. (2) And they stood in front of the cave, and a bright cloud overshadowed the cave. And the midwife said, "My soul is magnified today, because my eyes have seen something wonderful. Salvation has been born to Israel!"

And immediately the cloud withdrew from the cave, and a great light appeared in the cave, so that their eyes couldn't bear it. And a little later, the light withdrew until an infant appeared. And he came and took the breast of his mother, Mary.

And the midwife cried out and said, "How great today is for me, that I've seen this new miracle!"

(3) And the midwife went out from the cave, and Salome met her.

And she said to her, "Salome, Salome, I have to describe a new sight to you. A virgin has given birth, which is against her nature!"

And Salome said, "As the Lord my God lives, unless I examine her condition, I won't believe that the virgin has given birth."

Chapter 20: Salome's Examination

(1) And the midwife went in and said, "Mary, position yourself, because there's no small test coming concerning you."

And Salome examined her. And Salome cried out and said, "Woe because of my lawlessness and my unbelief! Because I've tested the living God, and look! My hand is on fire and falling away from me!"

(2) And she dropped to her knees before the Lord, saying, "God of my ancestors, remember me, that I've descended from Abraham, Isaac, and Jacob. Don't make an example of me to the people of Israel, but give me the back to the poor, because you know, Lord, that in your name I've healed people, and I've received my wages from you."

(3) And look! An angel of the Lord appeared, saying to her, "Salome, Salome, the Lord of All has heard your prayer. Bring your hand to the child and lift him up, and you'll receive salvation and joy."

(4) And Salome joyfully went to the child and lifted him up, saying, "I worship him, because a great king has been born to Israel." And immediately Salome was healed, and she left the cave justified.

And look! A voice was saying, "Salome, Salome, don't report the wonderful things you've seen until the child comes into Jerusalem."

Chapter 21: The Magi

(1) And look! Joseph prepared to go out into Judea when a great commotion arose in Bethlehem of Judea. For magi came, saying, "Where is the king of the Jews? For we saw his star in the East and have come to worship him."

(2) And when Herod heard, he was disturbed, and he sent officers to the magi, and sent for the chief priests and questioned them in his palace, saying to them, "What has been written about the Christ? Where will he be born?"

They said to him, "In Bethlehem of Judea, for this is what's written." And he set them (the chief priests) free.

And he questioned the magi, saying to them, "What sign did you see about the one who's been born king?"

And the magi said, "We saw an immense star shining among the other stars and dimming them so much that they weren't even visible. And so we knew that a king had been born for Israel, and we came to worship him."

And Herod said to them, "Go and search, and if you find him, report to me so that I can also come and worship him."

(3) And the magi went, and look! The star they had seen in the East led them until they came to the cave, and it stood over the head of the cave. And when they saw him with his mother Mary, the magi took gifts from their bags: gold, and frankincense, and myrrh.

And having been warned by the angel not to go into Judea, they returned to their country by another way.

Chapter 22: The Slaughter of the Infants

(1) When Herod saw that he had been tricked by the magi, he was angry. He sent out his killers, telling them to kill all the infants two years old and younger.

(2) And when Mary heard that the infants were being killed, she was afraid. She took her child, wrapped him in cloths, and put him in a manger for cows.

(3) And when Elizabeth heard that John was sought, she took him up into the hills and looked around for somewhere to hide him, but there wasn't a hiding place. Then Elizabeth groaned and said, "Mountain of God, take a mother with her child," because Elizabeth was unable to go up higher. And immediately, the mountain split and took her, and a light shone through the mountain for her. For an angel of the Lord was with them, protecting them.

Chapter 23: The Murder of Zechariah

(1) But Herod asked for John and sent officers to Zechariah, saying to him, "Where are you hiding your son?"

But he replied, saying to them, "I'm a minister of God, and I sit in God's Temple. How should I know where my son is?"

(2) And his officers went away and reported all these things to Herod. And Herod was angry, and said, "His son is about to be king over Israel!"

And he sent his officers again, to say to him, "Tell me the truth. Where's your son? You know that your life is in my hand."

And the officers went away and reported these things to him.

(3) And Zechariah said, "I'm a martyr of God if you shed my blood, because the Lord will receive my spirit, since you'll be spilling innocent blood at the entrance of the Temple of the Lord."

And around daybreak, Zechariah was murdered, and the people of Israel didn't know that he was murdered.

Chapter 24: Mourning for Zechariah

(1) But at the hour of greeting, the priests came, and Zechariah didn't meet them to bless them as was customary. And the priests stood around for Zechariah, waiting to greet him with a blessing and to glorify the Most High God.

(2) But when he delayed, they were all afraid. But one of them gathered the courage to go into the sanctuary and saw blood clotted beside the altar of the Lord. And a voice was saying, "Zechariah has been murdered, and his blood won't be wiped away until his avenger comes!"

When he heard this saying, he was afraid, and he went and reported to the priests what he had seen and heard. (3) And they gathered their courage and went and saw what had taken place. And the panels of the Temple cried out, and they (the priests) ripped their clothes from top to bottom. And they didn't find his corpse, but they found his blood had turned to stone. And they were afraid, and they went out and reported to all the people that Zechariah had been murdered. And when all the tribes of the people heard, they mourned him and wept three days and three nights.

(4) And after three days, the priests held a council about who should replace Zechariah. And the lot fell to Simeon, for he was told by the Holy Spirit that he wouldn't see death until he saw the Christ in the flesh.

Chapter 25: Conclusion

(1) Now I, James, wrote this history in Jerusalem when there was a commotion over Herod's death. I went into the wilderness until the commotion in Jerusalem had died down. I was glorifying the Lord God, who gave me the wisdom to write this history.

(2) And grace will be with all who fear the Lord. Amen.

Text Notes

Chapter 5: *the plate worn by the priest.* Literally, "the leaf of the priest." Possibly a reference to the metal disk worn on the priest's forehead, as described in Exodus 28:36-38 and 39:30, 31. Cf. Ronald F. Hock, *The Infancy Gospels of James and Thomas* (Polebridge Press), 1995, p. 39.

Chapter 8: *pollute the sanctuary.* I.e., by menstruation.

Chapter 10: On the elite group of young women responsible for spinning the Temple veil, cf. Cf. Megan Nutzman, "Mary in the *Protoevangelium of James:* A Jewish Woman in the Temple?" *Greek, Roman, and Byzantine Studies* (2013), Vol. 53, pp. 563-570.

Chapter 11: *throne.* Other translations use the word "chair" for the Greek term here, but George Zervos argues that the Temple was the actual location of the original location of the annunciation here ("An Early Non-Canonical Annunciation Story," *Society of Biblical Literature 1997 Seminar Papers,* Vol. 36, pp. 677-679). Cf. also Michael Peppard, *The World's Oldest Church: Bible, Art, and Ritual at Dura-Europos, Syria* (Yale), 2016, p. 160.

Chapter 16: *the water of the Lord's rebuke.* A tradition stemming from Numbers 5:11-31. Cf. Nutzman, *op. cit.,* pp. 559-563.

Chapters 18 through 21: The earliest Greek manuscript, the Bodmer Papyrus V (dating to the late third or early fourth century), contains a much more abbreviated version of these chapters. Cf. Michel Testuz, *Papyrus Bodmer V: Nativité de Marie* (Bibliotheca Bodmeriana), 1958, pp. 102-113; Thomas A. Wayment, *The Text of the New Testament Apocrypha (100 – 400 CE)* (Bloomsbury T&T Clark), 2013, pp. 68-70, 273-276. Cf. also George Zervos, "Christmas with Salome," in Amy-Jill Levine and Maria Mayo Robbins, eds., *A Feminist Companion to Mariology* (T&T Clark), 2005, pp. 77-98.

Chapter 19: *unless I examine her condition.* This reading is well attested by several manuscripts. De Strycker selects another reading: *unless I insert my finger and examine her condition.* Some manuscripts read *unless I see.* Others use the word *hand* instead of *finger.* Cf. Émile de Strycker, *La Forme la plus ancienne du Protévangile de Jacques* (Société des Bollandistes), 1961, p. 158; Bart D. Ehrman and Zlatko Pleše, *The Apocryphal Gospels: Texts and Tranlsations* (Oxford University Press), 2011, p. 62; and George T. Zervos' edited article, "Caught in the Act: Mary and the Adulteress," pp. 26ff, on-line at http://people.uncw.edu/zervosg/Pr236/New%20236/Caught%20in%20the%20Act%20Final%20-%20Edited.pdf (last accessed August 7, 2019). Cf. p. 28, where Zervos writes that "the overwhelming witness of the [manuscript] tradition of the [Infancy Gospel of James] confirms ... the 'explicit Johannine parallel' [i.e., John 20:25] ... cannot be considered with any degree of certainty to be the original reading."

Chapter 20: *Salome examined her.* This reading is from the same manuscripts used for the reading in Chapter 19 noted above. Other readings include *Salome inserted her finger into her nature / condition, she inserted her hand into her, Salome examined her nature / condition,* and *she observed her.* Cf. de Strycker, *op. cit.,* p. 160; Ehrman and Pleše, *op. cit.,* p. 62. In personal correspondence dated October 11, 2018, Dr. Samuel Zinner comments on the word *examined (sēmeiōsōmai)* used here: "According to LSJ, *sēmeioō* can in a medical context mean primarily *note down, take notice of.* However, secondarily it can mean *diagnose,* and later *examine,* as in Paul of Aegina *Pragmateia* Book 6 ch. 96 (7th cent. CE), where a physician uses fingers to examine for fractured ribs."

Appendix B:
A Public Domain Version of
the Infancy Gospel of Thomas

This translation has been committed to the public domain. It may be freely copied and used, in whole or in part, changed or unchanged, for any purpose.

The Infancy Gospel of Thomas was originally written in the second century CE. Manuscripts of this Gospel exist in several languages, dating as early as the fifth century in Syriac. Scholars currently divide the Greek manuscripts into four recensions: Greek A, Greek B, Greek D, and Greek S. The earliest Greek manuscript (the Greek S recension) is Hagios Saba 259, dating to the eleventh century.

The translation presented here is based on this earliest Greek manuscript, except chapters 17 and 18, which aren't included in Greek S. By contrast, most translations are based on Tischendorf's nineteenth-century transcript of the Greek A recension. For more information about the available manuscript evidence, see Tony Burke, *De Infantia Iesu Evangelium Thomae Graece* (Brepols), 2010.

Symbols

( ) Editorial insertion
† † Editorial revision
< > Unintelligible word
[   ] Gap in the text

Chapter 1: Prologue

I, Thomas the Israelite, thought it necessary to make known to all the Gentile brothers (and sisters) all the things done by our Lord Jesus Christ in the village of Nazareth, after he was born in our region of Bethlehem. This is the beginning:

Chapter 2: Jesus Makes Sparrows

(1) The child Jesus was five years old. After it rained, he was playing at the ford of a flowing stream. And stirring up the dirty waters, he gathered them into pools, and he made them clean and excellent, ordering them by word alone – and not ordering them by a deed.

(2) Then, having taken soft clay from the mud, he formed twelve sparrows from it. But it was the Sabbath when he did these things, and many children were with him.

(3) But a certain Jew saw the child Jesus with the other children doing these things. He went to Joseph his father and slandered the child Jesus, saying that "he made clay on the Sabbath, which isn't permissible, and formed twelve sparrows."

(4) And Joseph went and rebuked him (Jesus), saying, "Why are you doing these things on the Sabbath?"

But Jesus clapped his hands, ordering the birds with a shout in front of all, and said, "Go, take flight like living beings!" And the sparrows, taking flight, went away squawking.

(5) And having seen this, the Pharisee was amazed, and he reported it to all his friends.

Chapter 3: Jesus Curses Annas' Son

(1) And the son of Annas the high priest said to him (Jesus), "Why are you doing such a thing on the Sabbath?" And having taken a willow twig, he destroyed the pools and drained the water which Jesus had gathered, and he dried up their gatherings.

(2) But having seen what had happened, Jesus said to him, "Your fruit (will have) no root, and your shoot will be withered like a scorched branch in a violent wind!"

(3) And immediately that child withered away.

Chapter 4: Jesus Curses a Careless Child

(1) From there he was going with his father Joseph, and someone running struck his shoulder. And Jesus said to him, "Cursed be you because of your leader!"

And immediately he died.

And the people who saw that he had died immediately cried out and said, "From where was this child born, that his word becomes deed?"

(2) And when the parents of the dead child saw what had happened, they blamed Joseph his father, saying, "From wherever you have this child, you can't live with us in this village. If you want to be here, teach him to bless and not to curse, because our child has been taken away from us."

Chapter 5: Joseph Confronts Jesus

(1) And Joseph said to Jesus, "Why do you say such things, and they suffer and hate us?"

And the child said to Joseph, "Since you know wise words, you're not ignorant of where they came from; †they were spoken about a five-year-old.† And they won't be raised, and these will receive their punishment."

And immediately those accusing him became blind.

(2) And Joseph took his (Jesus') ear and pulled hard.

(3) And Jesus said to him, "It's enough for you seek and find me, and not, beyond that, to scourge me by having taken on a natural ignorance. You haven't clearly seen me, why I'm yours. Look! I've been subdued before you."

Chapter 6: First Teacher, Zacchaeus

(1) A teacher named Zacchaeus (was) standing (there), hearing Jesus saying these things to his father Joseph, and he was very amazed.

(2) And he said to Joseph, "Come, give him (to me), brother, so that he may be taught letters, and so that he may know all knowledge, and learn to love those his own age, and honor old age and respect elders, so that he may acquire a yearning for children, teaching them in return."

(3) But Joseph said to the teacher, "And who can control this child and teach him? Don't think of him as a small person, brother."

But the teacher said, "Give him to me, brother, and don't let him concern you."

(4) And the child Jesus looked at them and said to the teacher this speech: "Being a teacher comes naturally to you, but you're a stranger to the name with which you're named, because I'm outside of you and I'm within you on account of the nobility of my birth in the flesh. But you, a lawyer, don't know the law."

And he said to Joseph, "When you were born, I existed, standing beside you so that as a father you may be taught a teaching by me which no one else knows or can teach. And you will bear the name of salvation."

(5) And the Jews cried out and said to him, "Oh new and incredible wonder! The child is perhaps five years old, and oh, what words he says! We've never known such words. No one – neither a lawyer nor a Pharisee – has spoken like this child."

(6) The child answered them and said, "Why are you amazed? Or rather, why don't you believe the things I've said to you? The truth is that I, who was created before this world, know accurately when you were born, and your fathers, and their fathers."

(7) And all the people who heard this were speechless, no longer able to talk to him. But he went up to them, skipped around, and said, "I was playing with you because I know you're small-minded, and amazed with small things."

(8) Now when they seemed comforted by the child's encouragement, the teacher said to his father, "Come, bring him into the school. I'll teach him letters."

And Joseph took his hand and led him into the school. And the teacher flattered him, brought him into the school, and Zacchaeus wrote the alphabet for him and began to teach him, saying the same letter frequently. But the child didn't answer him.

And the teacher became irritated and struck him on the head.

And the child became irritated and said to him, "I want to teach you rather than be taught by you, since I know the letters you're teaching more accurately. To me these things are like a noisy gong or a clanging cymbal that don't bring out the sound, nor the glory, nor the power of understanding."

(9) When the child's anger ceased, he said all the letters by himself, from the alpha to the omega, very skillfully. And looking straight at the teacher he said, "If you don't know the nature of the alpha, how can you teach another the beta? Hypocrite! If you know, first teach me the alpha, and then I will trust you to speak of the beta." Then he began to teach the teacher about the first element. And he couldn't say anything to him.

(10) While many listened, he said to the teacher, "Listen, Teacher, and understand the arrangement of the first element. Now, notice how it has sharp lines and a middle stroke, which you see pointing, standing with legs apart, coming together, going out, dragging behind, lifting up, dancing around, <...>, in triple rhythm, two-cornered, of the same form, of the same thickness, of the same family, raised, balanced, isometric, of equal proportions. These are the lines of the alpha."

Chapter 7: Zacchaeus' Lament

(1) When the teacher heard such good familiarity (and) such lines of the first letter Jesus talked about, he was baffled by such teaching and his defense. And the teacher said, "Woe is me! Woe is me! I've been baffled and am miserable. I've brought shame on myself, taking on this child.

(2) "Take (him) away from me, brother, because I can't bear his gaze, nor the clarity of his word. This child is simply not of this earth. He can even tame fire! Perhaps this child existed before the creation of the world. What kind of womb bore him? What kind of mother raised him? I don't know. Woe is me, brother! He stupefies me. My mind can't follow him. I've deceived myself, thrice-unhappy as I am. I thought to gain a disciple, and I'm found having a teacher.

(3) "Friends, I ponder my shame, old man that I am, that I've been defeated by a child. I should be cast out and die, or flee this village because of this child. I can't be seen any longer among everyone, especially those who saw that I was defeated by a very small child. But what can I say or tell anyone about the lines of the first element? The truth is that I don't know, friends, because I understand neither the beginning nor the end!

(4) "Therefore, brother Joseph, lead him away with salvation into your house, because this child is a great thing – whether a god or an angel or whatever else I might say – I don't know."

Chapter 8: Jesus' Response

(1) The child Jesus laughed and said, "Now may the barren bear fruit, the blind see, and the foolish in heart find understanding: that I'm here from above, so that I may deliver those below and call them up, just as the one who sent me to you has ordered me."

(2) And immediately all who had fallen under his curse were saved. And no one dared to provoke him from then on.

Chapter 9: Jesus Raises Zeno

(1) And again, after many days, Jesus was playing with other children on a certain roof of an upstairs room. But one of the children fell and died. And the other children saw this and went into their houses. And they left Jesus alone.

(2) And the parents of the child who had died came and accused Jesus, saying, "You pushed down our child!"

But Jesus said, "I didn't push him down."

(3) And they were raging and shouting. Jesus came down from the roof and stood beside the body and cried out in a loud voice, saying, "Zeno, Zeno" – because this was his name – "Rise and say whether I pushed you down."

And he rose and said, "No, sir."

And they saw and were amazed.

And again Jesus said to him, "Fall asleep!"

And the parents of the child praised God and worshipped the child Jesus.

In Hagios Saba 259 (the Greek S recension), this passage appears after Chapter 16.

Chapter 10: Jesus Heals a Woodcutter

(1) Again, a certain young man was splitting wood into equal parts. And he split the bottom of his foot, bled out, and died.

(2) A commotion arose, and Jesus ran there. Forcing his way through the crowd, he seized the stricken foot, and immediately it was healed. And he said to the young man, "Go, split your wood."

(3) And the crowds saw and were amazed and said, "For he saved many souls from death, and he will continue to save all the days of his life."

Chapter 11: Jesus Carries Water in his Cloak

(1) And the child Jesus was about seven years old, and his mother Mary sent him to fill up water. But there was a great crowd at the water cistern, and the pitcher was struck and broke.

(2) But Jesus spread out the cloak he was wearing, filled it with water, and carried it to his mother. And Mary saw what sign

Jesus had done. She kissed him, saying, "Lord, my God, bless our child," because they were afraid lest someone bewitch him.

Chapter 12: Miracle of the Harvest

(1) And at the time of the sowing, Joseph sowed seeds, and the child Jesus sowed one measure of wheat.

(2) And his father reaped a hundred great measures. And he gave graciously to the poor and the orphans. But Joseph took from Jesus' seeds.

Chapter 13: Miracle of the Bed

(1) Now he (Jesus) was about eight years old. And his father, being a carpenter who made ploughs and yokes, took a bed from a certain rich man so that he might make it very great and suitable. And one of the beams, called the (...), was shorter; it didn't have the (right) length. Joseph was grieved, and didn't know what to do.

The child came to his father and said, "Set down the two boards and line them up on your end."

(2) And Joseph did just as he said to him. And the child Jesus stood at the other end and seized the short board and stretched it. And he made it equal with the other board.

And he said to his father, "Don't grieve, but make whatever you want to."

And Joseph embraced and kissed him, saying, "Blessed am I, that God gave this child to me."

Chapter 14: Second Teacher

(1) And Joseph saw his (Jesus') wisdom and understanding. He didn't want him to be unacquainted with letters, but gave him over to another teacher.

And the teacher wrote the alphabet for him (Jesus) and said, "Say alpha."

(2) And the child said, "First you tell me what the beta is, and I'll tell you what the alpha is."

And the teacher became irritated and struck him. And Jesus cursed him, and the teacher fell and died.

(3) And the child went into his house to his parents, and Joseph called his (Jesus') mother and ordered her not to set him (Jesus) free from the house so that those who provoke him may not die.

Chapter 15: Third Teacher

(1) And after some days, again another teacher said to his (Jesus') father Joseph: "Come, brother, give him to me in the school so that with flattery I can teach him letters."

And Joseph said to him, "If you have courage, brother, take him with salvation."

And the teacher took the child by the hand and led him away with much fear and concern. And the child went gladly.

(2) And entering the school, he (Jesus) found a book lying on the lectern. And he took it, but he didn't read what was written in it, because it wasn't from God's law. But he opened his mouth and uttered words so impressive that the teacher seated opposite heard him very gladly and encouraged him so that he might say more. And the crowd standing there was amazed at his holy words.

(3) And Joseph ran quickly to the school, suspecting that this teacher was no longer inexperienced and suffered. But the teacher said to Joseph, "So that you know, brother, I indeed took your child as a disciple, but he's full of much grace and wisdom. Therefore, brother, lead him away with salvation into your house."

(4) And he (Jesus) said to the teacher, "Since you spoke correctly and testified correctly, the one struck down will also be saved because of you." And immediately that teacher also was saved. And taking the child, he (Joseph) led him (Jesus) away into his house.

Chapter 16: Jesus Heals James' Snakebite

(1) And James went into the grove to tie up sticks so that they might make bread. And Jesus went with him. And as they were gathering the sticks, a terrible snake bit James on his hand.

(2) And he was sprawled out and dying. And the child Jesus ran to James and blew on the bite, and immediately the bite was healed. And the beast was destroyed, and James was saved.

Hagios Saba 259 (the Greek S recension) lacks Chapters 17 and 18. Consequently, the two chapters presented here are based on the Greek A recension of manuscripts.

Chapter 17: Jesus Heals a Baby

(1) And after these things, in Joseph's neighborhood a certain baby was sick and died. And his mother wept very much.

But Jesus heard that there was great grief and commotion, and he ran quickly. And he found the child dead, touched his chest, and said, "I say to you, baby, don't die, but live, and be with your mother."

And he (the baby) looked up immediately and laughed. And he (Jesus) said to the mother, "Take your child, give him milk, and remember me."

(2) And the crowd standing there was amazed, and said, "The truth is, this child is a god or an angel, because his every word becomes a deed!"

And Jesus went away again and played with the children.

Chapter 18: Jesus Heals a Builder

(1) And after some time, a building was being constructed. There was a great commotion, and Jesus got up and went there.

And seeing a man lying dead, he (Jesus) seized his (the man's) hand and said, "I tell you, man, rise and do your work." And he (the man) immediately rose and worshipped him.

> (2) And the crowd saw and was amazed and said, "This child is from heaven, for he saved many souls from death, and he will continue to save all the days of his life."

Chapter 19: Jesus in the Temple

(1) And when Jesus was twelve years old, his parents went, according to custom, to Jerusalem for the festival of the Passover. But during their return, Jesus stayed behind in Jerusalem. And his parents didn't know.

(2) And assuming him to be in the traveling company, they went a day's journey and searched for him among their known relatives. And not finding him, they returned to Jerusalem and searched for him.

And after three days, they found him in the temple sitting in the middle of the teachers, and listening to them and questioning them. And those hearing him were surprised how he questioned the elders and explained the main points of the law and the riddles and the parables of the prophets.

(3) And his mother said to him, "Child, what have you done to us? Look, we've been searching for you in pain and grieving."

And Jesus said, "Why were you looking for me? Didn't you know that it's necessary for me to be in the place of my Father?"

(4) And the scribes and the Pharisees said to Mary, "You're the mother of this child?"

She said, "I am."

And they said to her, "Blessed are you that the Lord God has blessed the fruit of your womb, because we've never seen such wisdom of praise and glory of virtue."

(5) And Jesus stood up and followed his mother from there, and was obedient to his parents. And she treasured all these things, pondering them in her heart.

And Jesus advanced in wisdom and maturity and grace before God and humans. To whom be the [glory …].

Text Notes

Chapter 1: The prologue is probably not original. This Gospel nowhere else describes Jesus as "Lord" or "Christ" (except possibly in Chapter 9; cf. below). Typically he's designated either "Jesus" or "the child Jesus."

Chapters 3 and 4: Presumably these curses are reversed in 8.2, and the children are brought back to life.

Chapter 5: *they were spoken about a five-year-old.* Based on the reconstruction of Reidar Aasgaard, *The Childhood of Jesus: Decoding the Apocryphal Infancy Gospel of Thomas* (James Clarke & Co.), 2010, p. 221; these words are left untranslated by Tony Burke, *De Infantia Iesu Evangelium Thomae Graece* (Brepols), 2010, p. 306.

Chapter 6: *I, who was created before this world.* An allusion to Wisdom in Proverbs 8:22 (correspondence with Samuel Zinner dated December 18, 2018). Aasgaard (*op. cit.,* pp. 142, 236) renders this phrase as *"I – and he <who existed> before this world was created." [...]* This word is unintelligible in the Greek. Cf. Burke, *op. cit.,* pp. 318, 319.

Chapter 9: *"Zeno, Zeno" – because this was his name.* Likely an allusion to one of the prominent philosophers (correspondence with Samuel Zinner dated December 18, 2018). In the later Greek recensions, Jesus doesn't instruct Zeno to "fall asleep" again. *"No, sir."* The word for "sir" *(kyrios)* could also mean "Lord" or "Master." Other translations choose "Lord."

Chapter 13: *"called the (…)."* One or more words appear to have been omitted from Hagios Saba 259 (the Greek S recension).

Chapter 15: *And immediately that teacher also was saved.* The second teacher, from chapter 14.

Chapters 17 and 18: For the the Greek A recension of manuscripts, cf. Constantin von Tischendorf, *Evangelia Apocrypha* (2nd ed.; Leipzig: Mendelssohn), 1876, pp. 140-157, in Rick Brannan, *Greek Apocryphal Gospels, Fragments & Agrapha: Texts and Transcriptions* (Lexham Press), 2013; Bart D. Ehrman and Zlatko Pleše, *The Apocryphal Gospels: Texts and Translations* (Oxford University Press), 2011.

Chapter 18: *a building was being constructed.* Burke proposes that a line of text describing the worker falling has been accidentally omitted. Cf. Burke, *op. cit.,* p. 384, n.1. The Greek D recension of manuscripts describe "a certain builder" falling and dying. Cf. Burke, *op. cit.,* pp. 444, 445.

Notes

Introduction

[1]Philip Wegmann, "Alabama state auditor defends Roy Moore against sexual allegations, invokes Mary and Joseph," *Washington Examiner,* November 9, 2017, on-line at https://www.washingtonexaminer.com/alabama-state-auditor-defends-roy-moore-against-sexual-allegations-invokes-mary-and-joseph. Last accessed June 16, 2019.

[2]Paolo Piria and Russell Kagan (Producers) and Roger Young (Director), *Jesus* [Motion Picture] (United States: Five Mile River Films, Ltd.), 199

[3]Christopher A. Frilingos, *Jesus, Mary, and Joseph: Family Trouble in the Infancy Gospels* (University of Pennsylvania Press), 2017, p. 3.

[4]Bettina Eltrop and Claudia Janssen, "Protevangelium of James: God's Story Goes On," in Luise Schottroff and Marie-Theres Wacker, eds., *Feminist Biblical Interpretation: A Compendium of Critical Commentary on the Books of the Bible and Related Literature,* (Eerdmans), 2012, p. 995.

[5]Cf. Samuel Zinner, "The Infancy Gospels of James and Thomas and the Canonical Gospels in Conversation with Josephus: Reconstructing Historical Backgrounds – Assessing Literary Parallels," forthcoming in the *Journal of Higher Criticism Supplement Series,* p. 44: "We might then view [Infancy James'] central interest in the temple as congruent with a revival of interest in the temple and its rebuilding in the years leading up to the Bar Kokhba

Revolt, and to an extent thereafter, since the quashing of the revolt would not have immediately ended all hopes for an eschatologically renewed temple."

Chapter One

[1]Wilhelm Schneemelcher, ed., and McL. Wilson, R. (trans.), *New Testament Apocrypha, Vol. 1: Gospels and Related Writings* (Westminster John Knox Press), 1991, pp. 421, 422.

[2]*Ibid.,* p. 423.

[3]C.f. H.R. Smid, *Protevangelium Jacobi: A Commentary*, trans. by G.E. Van Baaren-Pape (Van Gorcum), 1965, p. 22: "On the whole we may say that [it] was possibly written in Syria but that the evidence is not conclusive." Cf. also Jane Schaberg, "The Infancy of Mary of Nazareth," in Elisabeth Schüssler Fiorenza, ed., *Searching the Scriptures, Volume Two: A Feminist Commentary* (Crossroad), 1994, p. 718.

[4]Cf. Ronald F. Hock, *The Infancy Gospels of James and Thomas* (Polebridge Press), 1995, p. 4.

[5]Zinner, *op. cit.,* p. 46.

[6]*Ibid.,* pp. 48, 49.

[7]On the latter point, cf. Zinner, *ibid.*; Eltrop and Janssen, *op. cit.,* p. 992.

[8]Eltrop and Janssen, *op. cit.,* p. 991.

[9]*Ibid.*

[10]Megan Nutzman, "Mary in the *Protoevangelium of James:* A Jewish Woman in the Temple?" *Greek, Roman, and Byzantine Studies* (2013), Vol. 53, pp. 571-578. Cf. also Ally Kateusz, *Mary and Early Christian Women: Hidden Leadership* (Palgrave Macmillan), 2019, p. 5.

[11]Zinner, *op. cit.,* p. 17.

[12]*Ibid.,* pp. 13, 14. Interestingly, he notes the language of "avenging" rather than "judging" aligns more closely with the Hebrew text than with the Greek Septuagint.

[13]*Ibid.,* p. 15.

[14]The examples in this paragraph are from correspondence with Samuel Zinner on October 5 and 6, 2018.

[15]Cf. Nutzman, *op. cit.,* p. 555, n. 8.

[16]Frilingos, *op. cit.,* p. 57. It may be noted, however, that manuscripts vary considerably in this part of the text, suggesting editorial changes regarding Salome's violation of Mary to prove Mary's postpartum virginity. For differing redaction theories, cf. George Zervos, "Christmas with Salome," in *A Feminist Companion to Mariology,* ed. Amy-Jill Levine and Maria Mayou Robb (T&T Clark), 2005; Mark M. Mattison, "Responsible Midwifery or Reckless Disbelief? Revisiting Salome's Examination of Mary in *The Protevangelium Jacobi,*" presented on May 12, 2019 at the 54th International Congress on Medieval Studies, publication forthcoming.

[17]Cf. Zinner, *op. cit.,* p. 26.

[18]Eric M. Vanden Eykel, *"But Their Faces Were All Looking Up": Author and Reader in the Protevangelium of James,* (T&T Clark), 2016, pp. 158-162. This connection was also suggested to me in

personal correspondence from Samuel Zinner dated October 6, 2018. Interestingly, a related narrative from a Sahidic Coptic fragment of The Life of the Virgin describes the cave as a "tomb"; cf. Forbes Robinson, *Coptic Apocryphal Gospels* (Cambridge University Press), 1896, pp. 196, 197.

[19]Schaberg, *op. cit.*, p. 724. Cf. Also Eltrop and Jannsen, *op. cit.*, p. 990.

[20]*Ibid.*, p. 718.

Chapter Three

[1]Cf. Schneemelcher, *op. cit.*, pp. 439-441.

[2]Cf. Zinner, *op. cit.*, pp. 62-64.

[3]*Ibid.*, pp. 70-74.

[4]*Ibid.*, p. 98.

[5]Jacob Neusner, "Zaccheus/Zakkai," *The Harvard Theological Reivew,* (1964), Vol. 57, No. 1, pp. 57, 58.

[6]Cf. Zinner, *op. cit.*, pp. 54, 57, 71.

[7]*Ibid.*, p. 98.

[8]Specifically, Zinner writes that "In the mind of [Infancy Thomas'] author, Jesus was not responsible for any misdeeds committed before age thirteen – not even murder! The relevant ancient Jewish sources do not even raise the possibility that children could commit such heinous criminal deeds" (*ibid.*).

[9]Reidar Aasgaard, *The Childhood of Jesus: Decoding the Apocryphal Infancy Gospel of Thomas* (James Clarke & Co.), 2010, pp. 152-157.

[10]*Ibid.,* p. 165.

[11]Cf. Tony Burke, *De Infantia Iesu Evangelium Thomae Graece* (Brepols), 2010, p. 302.

[12]Cf. Zinner, *op. cit.,* p. 66, n. 146.

[13]*Ibid.,* p. 105.

[14]Cf. Aasgaard, *op. cit.,* p. 128.

[15]Cf. Zinner, *op. cit.,* pp. 51ff.

Bibliography

Aasgaard, Reidar, *The Childhood of Jesus: Decoding the Apocryphal Infancy Gospel of Thomas* (James Clarke & Co.), 2010

Burke, Tony, *De Infantia Iesu Evangelium Thomae Graece* (Brepols), 2010

de Strycker, Émile, *La Forme la plus ancienne du Protévangile de Jacques* (Société des Bollandistes), 1961

Ehrman, Bart D. and Pleše, Zlatko, *The Apocryphal Gospels: Texts and Translations* (Oxford University Press), 2011

Eltrop, Bettina and Janssen, Claudia, "Protevangelium of James: God's Story Goes On," in Luise Schottroff and Marie-Theres Wacker, eds., *Feminist Biblical Interpretation: A Compendium of Critical Commentary on the Books of the Bible and Related Literature,* (Eerdmans), 2012

Frilingos, Christopher A., *Jesus, Mary, and Joseph: Family Trouble in the Infancy Gospels* (University of Pennsylvania Press), 2017

Hock, Ronald F., *The Infancy Gospels of James and Thomas* (Polebridge Press), 1995

Kateusz, Ally, *Mary and Early Christian Women: Hidden Leadership* (Palgrave Macmillan), 2019

Mattison, Mark M., "Responsible Midwifery or Reckless Disbelief? Revisiting Salome's Examination of Mary in *The Protevangelium Jacobi*," presented on May 12, 2019 at the 54th International Congress on Medieval Studies, publication forthcoming.

Neusner, Jacob, "Zaccheus/Zakkai," *The Harvard Theological Reivew* (1964), Vol. 57, No. 1, pp. 57-59

Nutzman, Megan, "Mary in the *Protoevangelium of James:* A Jewish Woman in the Temple?" *Greek, Roman, and Byzantine Studies* (2013), Vol. 53, pp. 563-570

Peppard, Michael, *The World's Oldest Church: Bible, Art, and Ritual at Dura-Europos, Syria* (Yale), 2016

Piria, Paolo, and Kagan, Russell, (Producers) and Young, Roger (Director). *Jesus* [Motion Picture] (United States: Five Mile River Films, Ltd.), 1999

Robinson, Forbes, *Coptic Apocryphal Gospels* (Cambridge University Press), 1896

Schaberg, Jane, "The Infancy of Mary of Nazareth," in Elisabeth Schüssler Fiorenza, ed., *Searching the Scriptures, Volume Two: A Feminist Commentary* (Crossroad), 1994

Schneemelcher, Wilhelm, ed., and McL. Wilson, R. (trans.), *New Testament Apocrypha. Vol. 1: Gospels and Related Writings* (Westminster John Knox Press), 1991

Smid, H.R., *Protevangelium Jacobi: A Commentary*, trans. by G.E. Van Baaren-Pape (Van Gorcum), 1965

Testuz, Michel, *Papyrus Bodmer V: Nativité de Marie* (Bibliotheca Bodmeriana), 1958

Vanden Eykel, Eric M., *"But Their Faces Were All Looking Up"*: *Author and Reader in the Protevangelium of James,* (T&T Clark), 2016

von Tischendorf, Constantin, *Evangelia Apocrypha* (2nd ed.; Leipzig: Mendelssohn), 1876, pp. 1–50, in Brannan, Rick, *Greek Apocryphal Gospels, Fragments & Agrapha: Texts and Transcriptions* (Lexham Press), 2013

Wayment, Thomas A., *The Text of the New Testament Apocrypha (100 – 400 CE)* (Bloomsbury T&T Clark), 2013

Wegmann, Philip, "Alabama state auditor defends Roy Moore against sexual allegations, invokes Mary and Joseph," *Washington Examiner,* November 9, 2017, on-line at https://www.washingtonexaminer.com/alabama-state-auditor-defends-roy-moore-against-sexual-allegations-invokes-mary-and-joseph. Last accessed June 16, 2019.

Zervos, George, "An Early Non-Canonical Annunciation Story," *Society of Biblical Literature 1997 Seminar Papers,* Vol. 36, pp. 677-679

Zervos, George, "Christmas with Salome," in Amy-Jill Levine and Maria Mayo Robbins, eds., *A Feminist Companion to Mariology* (T&T Clark), 2005, pp. 77-98

Zervos, George T., "Caught in the Act: Mary and the Adulteress," pp. 26ff, on-line at http://people.uncw.edu/zervosg /Pr236/New%20236/Caught%20in%20the%20Act%20Final% 20-%20Edited.pdf. Last accessed August 7, 2019.

Zinner, Samuel, "The Infancy Gospels of James and Thomas and the Canonical Gospels in Conversation with Josephus: Reconstructing Historical Backgrounds – Assessing Literary Parallels," forthcoming in the *Journal of Higher Criticism Supplement Series*

Made in the USA
Las Vegas, NV
11 August 2022

53137050R00049